ROBERT H. JACKSON

Robert H. Jackson

New Deal Lawyer
Supreme Court Justice
Nuremberg Prosecutor

GAIL JARROW

CALKINS CREEK
Honesdale, Pennsylvania

LIBRARY OF CONGRESS CATALOGING-IN-PUBLICATION DATA
Jarrow, Gail.
Robert H. Jackson : New Deal lawyer,
Supreme Court Justice, Nuremberg prosecutor / by Gail Jarrow.
p. cm.
Includes bibliographical references and index.
ISBN 978-1-59078-511-9 (hardcover : alk. paper)
1. Jackson, Robert Houghwout, 1892–1954—Juvenile literature.
2. Judges—United States—Biography—Juvenile literature.
3. United States. Supreme Court—Biography—Juvenile literature. I. Title.
KF8745.J27J37 2008
347.73'2634—dc22
[B]
2007018858

CALKINS CREEK
An Imprint of Boyds Mills Press, Inc.
815 Church Street
Honesdale, Pennsylvania 18431

In memory of my grandparents. Along with Robert H. Jackson, they were part of a remarkable generation that lived through two world wars and several smaller ones, the Great Depression, and unprecedented changes in society and technology. Through it all, they never gave up trying to make the world a better place for their children and grandchildren.

—G.J.

ACKNOWLEDGMENTS

Special thanks go to the Robert H. Jackson Center in Jamestown, New York, for its help throughout the project. Gregory L. Peterson provided crucial reference materials and useful comments along the way. Eric Larson helped with research and reviewed the final manuscript. Rolland Kidder and Carol Drake offered suggestions and assistance.

John Q. Barrett, Professor of Law at St. John's University and the Elizabeth S. Lenna Fellow at the Jackson Center, graciously shared his expertise by answering my questions, recommending sources, and giving me valuable feedback on the manuscript.

In addition, the Jackson Center generously provided photographs from its collection, including family pictures donated by Harold Jackson Adams, Robert H. Jackson's nephew, and photographs taken by Ray D'Addario, official photographer at the Nuremberg Trial. Thanks to Linda Cowan, who gathered these images for me.

I was also fortunate to have the assistance of the following people: Dr. Daun van Ee, from the Manuscript Division, Library of Congress; Rosemary Newnham and David Loerke, from Columbia University's Oral History Research Office; Sylvia Lobb and the staff at the Fenton History Center Museum and Library in Jamestown, New York; June Burgett, historian for Frewsburg, New York; Mark Renovitch, at the Franklin D. Roosevelt Library; Pauline Testerman, at the Harry S. Truman Library; Jennifer Carpenter and Steve Petteway, from the Curator's Office of the Supreme Court; Philip Brumley, from the legal department of the Watch Tower Bible and Tract Society; and David Anderson, of Streetwise Creative Group.

I'm grateful to Kent L. Brown Jr., who kindled my interest in Jackson; and to Helen Robinson, Joan Hyman, Jill Goodman, and Jeryl Genschow, who turned my manuscript into a book.

I particularly appreciate the advice, guidance, and support of my talented editor, Carolyn P. Yoder.

Finally, for his patience as I spent months immersed in Robert Houghwout Jackson's life, I thank another exceptional Robert.

—G.J.

CONTENTS

ONE   He Speaks for the World   9

TWO   Country Boy   12

THREE   "Mark You Jackson"   21

FOUR   Legal Eagle   27

FIVE   New Deal Lawyer   37

SIX   Ambitions and Promises   47

SEVEN   The Eloquent Justice   59

EIGHT   The Case Against the Nazis   70

NINE   The Nuremberg Trial   79

TEN   A Riot, a Strike, and an Eight-Year-Old Girl   95

ELEVEN   His Words Live On   106

Timeline   112

Notes   114

Bibliography   118

For More Information   122

Index   124

Picture Credits   128

The Ruins of World War II
The fighting in Europe during World War II destroyed many cities and killed millions of soldiers and civilians. This is Nuremberg, Germany, after the war ended in 1945.

CHAPTER ONE

He Speaks for the World

The courtroom in Nuremberg became quiet as the middle-aged man stepped to the lectern. Dressed in a dark suit with white handkerchief in the breast pocket, Robert H. Jackson grasped the sides of the wooden podium. He glanced down at the sheets of legal-sized white paper and took a deep breath. This speech would be the most important he had ever made.

World War II had finally ended after six bloody years. Tens of millions of soldiers and civilians were dead. Europe lay in ruins. Twenty of the men responsible for that horror stared at Jackson from the prisoners' dock. It was his job to bring these German Nazi leaders to justice.

The victorious Allies—the Americans, British, French, and Soviets—had set up the International Military Tribunal in the German city to try the defeated Nazis. Never before had the leaders of a nation been put on trial for war crimes.

Jackson agreed to become chief U.S. prosecutor at the trial because he wanted to be part of this momentous event. He hadn't expected the vast amount of time and effort the job would require. For the past seven months, the Allies had clashed about how to conduct the trial, and Jackson found that the "discords were stubborn and deep."

Now as the trial began, he wished that the Allies' case were more organized. The amount of evidence against the Nazi leaders—one hundred thousand documents and twenty-five thousand photographs—was staggering. Jackson and his team of lawyers and investigators had rushed their preparation so that the trial wouldn't be delayed any longer. The public was impatient for revenge against the Nazis. Many in the United States and Europe even called for the prisoners to be executed without a trial.

Jackson knew it was on his shoulders to show the world that this trial would be fair. His opening address had to make that clear. For weeks he worked on the speech, going through so many revisions that he lost count. The writing had been "a long, hard, grinding job." But he was inspired as he wrote, and he felt confident in the words he had chosen.

Jackson spoke into the microphone, his voice strong and determined: "The privilege of opening the first trial in history for crimes against the peace of the world imposes a grave responsibility. The wrongs which we seek to condemn and punish have been so calculated, so malignant, and so devastating, that civilization cannot tolerate their being ignored, because it cannot survive their being repeated."

Bright lights illuminated the crowded courtroom so that cameras could film the trial. Jackson noticed that some people, including a few of the Nazi defendants, wore sunglasses to shield their eyes.

He continued, trying to speak slowly enough for interpreters to translate his words into German, French, and Russian. "These prisoners represent sinister influences that will lurk in the world long after their bodies have returned to dust. We will show them to be living symbols of racial hatreds, of terrorism and violence, and of the arrogance and cruelty of power."

For four hours on November 21, 1945, Robert Jackson outlined the Allies' case against the high-ranking Nazis. His speech was recorded on film and audiotape, and the international press reported on it. The world watched and listened.

Less than a dozen years before, the man who held the world's attention had been a country lawyer. As a boy, he mowed fields and cared for horses in his father's livery stable. He spent not a single day in college, and he did not have a law degree.

A remarkable journey had taken Jackson from a New York farmhouse to the Nuremberg courtroom. The path led him to a president's inner circle, to the attorney general's seat in the cabinet, and to the Supreme Court bench.

While a member of President Franklin Delano Roosevelt's administration, Jackson worked on the New Deal program to lift the country from the Great

Chief American Prosecutor
Robert H. Jackson addresses
the court at the Nuremberg War
Crimes Trial in 1945.

Depression of the 1930s. As attorney general, he helped prepare the nation for World War II. As a Supreme Court justice, Jackson was involved in Court rulings that changed American society. His planning for the Nuremberg Trial laid the groundwork for modern international law.

During his lifetime, Jackson was admired for his sense of fairness and his skill with words. Many assumed that he would be a presidential candidate or chief justice of the Supreme Court.

Despite his ambitions, some dreams remained unfulfilled. Events and other people stood in the way. His skin was perhaps too thin for the personal attacks that are part of fierce political battles. Yet by the time Robert Houghwout Jackson died in 1954, he had left his mark on the country and the world.

CHAPTER TWO

Country Boy

Spring Creek Farmhouse
Robert Jackson was born in this house, built next to the Brokenstraw Creek in northwestern Pennsylvania by his great-grandfather Elijah Jackson.

Snowdrifts blocked the roads and covered the fields around William E. Jackson's Pennsylvania farmhouse. His wife, Angelina, was in labor with their first child. William didn't know how long he had before the baby arrived. Wasting no time, he hitched up his horse to a sleigh and drove six miles to fetch the doctor.

Before the day ended on February 13, 1892, Robert Houghwout Jackson had been born. "I let out a cry of relief," Jackson wrote fifty years later. "It was over and I would never have that to go through again."

The United States was changing into an industrial nation of factories, large companies, and growing cities. But rural Spring Creek, Pennsylvania, remained much the way it had been when Robert's great-grandfather Elijah built the farmhouse next to Brokenstraw Creek.

Elijah Jackson was one of the first settlers in the forests of northwestern Pennsylvania near Lake Erie after the Revolutionary War. He and his sons cut down trees on the farm and sold the lumber. After Elijah's death, his bachelor son William Miles Jackson took over the farm.

Angelina Houghwout Jackson, *Robert's mother. Jackson later described her as a calm and serene woman.*

By the time William Miles was in his seventies, he needed help running the farm. He invited his newlywed nephew, William, and wife, Angelina, to move in with him.

William Eldred Jackson and Angelina Houghwout* had met as students at the same rural school. They both grew up on farms and welcomed the chance to work one on their own.

Their son's birth marked the third generation born in the Jackson farmhouse. Like most Americans in those days, Robert was a mix of European ancestors—English, Scotch, Irish, and Dutch. Many relatives from both sides of his family still lived close to Spring Creek.

While William and Angelina were busy with farm work, Robert's great-uncle William Miles took care of him. "As soon as my legs would carry me," Jackson recalled, "I many times walked the old Spring Creek farm over with him."

Uncle William showed Robert the springs where they could get a fresh, cold drink of water. He entertained his nephew with stories about the Indians living in the area when the Jacksons first settled there.

As they strolled along the Brokenstraw Creek, Uncle William told of his adventures taking lumber from the farm down the creek on a raft to the Allegheny River. Robert loved hearing how Uncle William had piloted the raft all the way to Pittsburgh to sell the lumber, then hiked more than a hundred miles back home.

Uncle William had been Spring Creek's justice of the peace for thirty years, and neighbors regularly came by the house for legal advice. Robert first heard about courts and trials from him.

Robert and his sister Ella, two years younger, were expected to help their

*Sometimes spelled *Houghwot* by the family.

mother. "We did as we were told," he said, "because there was a kind of leadership about her—she didn't drive us."

Robert collected wood for the stove, churned butter, weeded the garden, and fed the chickens and hogs. He knew how to do the milking, but he tried to get out of that chore. He didn't like cows and much preferred horses.

When Robert was five, his father decided that he couldn't earn a good living from the farm anymore. The best timber had been cut down and there wasn't enough lumber to sell. William had plans for running a business.

He set his eye on Frewsburg, New York, thirty miles north of Spring Creek. The village of about five hundred people had dirt streets, wooden sidewalks, and a railroad station. The railroad brought visitors, and visitors needed a place to stay. William saw a business opportunity.

He renovated the hotel and renamed it Hotel Jackson. Next door, he ran a livery stable where people could rent horse-drawn carriages or board horses. William invested in real estate, too. He bought houses, fixed them up, and sold them for profit.

The Jackson family—including Uncle William, who lived with them until his death in 1899—moved into the hotel. The family stayed there for a few years until settling into a two-story house in Frewsburg.

After living on the farm, Robert thought the village was exciting. Local farmers drove their horse-drawn wagons into town to visit the stores and businesses, and trains passed through. He had fun running, playing, and exploring it all with his friends.

Robert helped his father feed and clean the horses at the livery stable. "I had a pony from the time I could stay on one," he wrote later. He owned and rode horses his entire life.

William Eldred Jackson, Robert's father (pictured in the small photo below), stands in front of his livery stable with one of his horses. He was an accomplished horse breeder.

Frewsburg School
Jackson attended this school from first grade through high school. Students pose out front in this undated photograph.

William E. Jackson had a passion for breeding fast racehorses, and he was good at it. Robert sometimes tagged along on his father's trips to buy and sell horses. When William entered his horses in trotting races in the area, Robert went with him. He slept in the stalls with the horses, rubbed them down, and helped to train them.

But William Jackson made clear that he didn't want Robert to make a career of racing or breeding. His son could do better than that. Maybe he'd be a doctor.

When Robert was six, he started first grade at the school in Frewsburg. The school had a library, an assembly hall, and four classrooms. All grades through high school met in the two-story building, with several grades grouped together in each classroom.

Every morning Robert and his schoolmates gathered in the assembly hall to sing songs, including a hymn. They listened to a Bible reading and recited the Lord's Prayer.

Robert never thought the schoolwork was very hard. He earned good grades, especially if he liked the subject and wanted to learn more about it. His older cousin Lena used to say that he asked "more questions than any other 10 boys."

His favorite subject was history. Robert's fourth-grade teacher, Mrs. Mackie,

The Jackson Family, around 1902. William, Ella, Robert, and Angelina. Robert's youngest sister, Helen, was born in 1904.

recalled, "One of his hobbies was to name the presidents of the United States in proper order with their dates."

The Jacksons enjoyed reading, and so did Robert. His mother read stories to the children every night. William Jackson read the newspaper aloud to his family.

The local doctor, Thomas Jefferson Whitney, encouraged Robert to read, too. Robert sometimes rode in the doctor's carriage on his rounds to see patients. When the doctor stopped at a patient's house, Robert held the horse. During their rides together, Dr. Whitney discussed books.

Robert read his way through most of the five hundred books in Frewsburg's library. For all of his life, Jackson read whenever he could—biography, history, political science, law, and philosophy. Often he made notes in the book margins.

His love of reading helped Robert stand out in school. His principal, George Raynor, commented that he was "a perfectly normal boy with an unusually keen mind."

One teacher wrote on Robert's report card: "Enthusiastic student. Doing excellent work."

While he was growing up, Robert frequently visited his grandparents. "My parents were busy," he said, "while the older people were more free and welcomed my company. ... I spent much more time perhaps with my grandparents than I did with my parents."

His Jackson grandparents retired from their farm in Pennsylvania and moved to Frewsburg, two doors down the street from their son's house. Robert felt especially close to his grandmother Mary Eldred Jackson. She read poetry to him, and he enjoyed the rhythm of the words and her soft voice, even when he was too young to understand what the poems meant.

During the summers, Robert stayed at the farm in Pennsylvania where his mother had grown up, about twenty miles south of Frewsburg. His grandmother Parthena Gregory Houghwout was a widow, but she still ran the farm. Robert helped with the summer work. He cut the hay by driving the horse team that pulled the mower.

Robert spent hours exploring Grandma Houghwout's farm and the woods outside of Frewsburg. He set out on these adventures by himself, hiking with his dog or riding a horse. Sometimes he took a gun to hunt small game or a pole to fish in a creek. "I never hunted or fished with very much concern about what I got," he said. "I like[d] the walk and the trip through the woods. That's what interested me most."

Parthena Gregory Houghwout, *Robert's widowed grandmother, lived and worked on her Pennsylvania farm until her death. As a boy, Robert helped with farm chores during the summers.*

When Robert was twelve, his sister Helen was born. That same year Grandmother Mary Jackson died, and Grandfather Robert R. Jackson moved in with Robert's family. Grandfather Jackson was full of fascinating stories, just as his brother (Uncle William) had been. He told Robert about hiking across the Isthmus of Panama before the Panama Canal was built, sailing to California in 1850 during the gold rush, and finding gold.

Grandfather Jackson was interested in politics and world affairs. He talked to Robert about what he read in his many American and European history books and in the daily newspapers. The Jacksons had different political views from the rest of the Republican-voting community. Grandfather Jackson was proud that "he first voted for Franklin Pierce [in 1852] and had voted for every Democratic candidate for President from that time down. ..."

In Frewsburg and other rural areas of the North, Democrats had been unpopular for more than forty years. In the years before the

Robert Rutherford Jackson, *Robert's grandfather, moved in with the Jackson family when Robert was twelve. Grandfather Jackson was well read and interested in politics.*

Civil War, people thought the Democratic Party had favored the Southern cotton planters and defended slavery. After the Southern states seceded, many Democrats had not supported the war.

Grandfather Jackson told Robert that he was against war in general and the Civil War in particular. He thought that the antislavery abolitionists and the slave owners were both hotheaded groups that pushed the country into war. When he was drafted, he paid a substitute to fight for him. Grandfather Jackson's antiwar views stuck with Robert.

Sometimes Robert went to the Frewsburg general store with his grandfather. He listened as a dozen or more men gathered around the wood-burning stove to gossip and argue about the state of the country.

Since the Civil War, industries such as railroads, banking, and steel had grown and were controlled by only a few powerful companies. Many people thought these businesses

Frewsburg, New York, *in 1908, when Robert was sixteen. The streets were unpaved, and people still traveled by horse and carriage.*

were too big. They wanted the government to stop the companies from taking advantage of smaller businesses, farmers, and workers. Unions were organizing and going on strike against the companies.

The Frewsburg men had opinions about all of it. To Robert, the discussions were "free-for-alls." He noticed how Grandfather Jackson spoke his mind and never lost his temper. Robert admired how he argued with his neighbors while keeping their friendship.

The Jacksons had different ideas from their neighbors about religion, too. They read the Bible but weren't church members. Robert and his sister attended Sunday school at the nearby Baptist church because their friends went there.

One evening Robert and some friends sneaked into a revival meeting. Often held in the Frewsburg area, revivals were religious services full of intense emotion. By pretending they had come to be saved from their sins, the boys made fun of the people at the revival. "They [the people] knew it was a lie. It was a decidedly sour note in the meeting," Jackson said later.

By the next morning, William Jackson had heard about it. At the breakfast table, he scolded his son for being disrespectful. Robert got the message. "I was always taught to respect other people's religion and never to start a religious argument."

———✦———

Robert's family had no patience for laziness. It seemed to him that they all liked work, and they expected him to like it, too. When he was twelve and old enough to be hired, Robert found a job at the local canning factory during the harvest season. In his first summer there, he earned seventy-five cents—about seventeen dollars today—for every ten-hour day he worked pushing pea pods into the podding machine.

"I do not think that I ever received more than 10¢ an hour," Jackson recalled. "Nor was fourteen hours of working time unusual on Saturdays during the rush season." But he didn't mind. Many of his friends worked there, and that made it more fun.

When they weren't working or going to school, Robert and his friends had picnics and ice-cream socials. In the fall, they collected chestnuts and hickory nuts. When the weather was cold, they skated on the creek and went sleigh riding. In the spring, they boiled maple syrup into sugar.

Robert was always looking for the

Robert Jackson's Family, around 1907–1908. Sitting: Robert, sister Ella, Grandfather Robert R. Jackson with sister Helen, an unidentified woman. Standing: An unidentified woman, father William, mother Angelina.

chance to play a prank. One warm spring day, he asked his teacher if he could get a drink of cool water from the bucket at the rear of the classroom. While he filled the dipper for a sip, he glanced out the open window. Two floors below, he spotted some men shoveling coal into the school basement.

This was too good to pass up! Robert waited for his teacher to turn her back. Then he poured the dipper full of water out the open window. One worker got a cold surprise down his neck. Swearing and screaming, the man vowed to catch the person who had done it. The whole school heard his shouts. By then, Robert was back at his desk, innocently studying a book.

Halloween was the best time for pranks. One year Robert and his friends tipped over outhouses. Another year they tied a quilt around the clapper of the school bell so that it couldn't ring to announce the beginning of classes.

Robert usually got away with his pranks, but not always. When he was fourteen, he was expelled from school. It started when Robert and some friends were socializing in the assembly room while they ate their lunches. A strict, unpopular teacher broke up their fun and made them sit in assigned seats during the lunch hour. To protest, Robert and the others paraded out of school.

Outside, they saw the sunny sky and the hard, smooth ice on the creek, so the group decided to spend the afternoon skating. Their protest had turned out to be a great idea.

But the idea didn't seem so great when they discovered that the teacher had expelled them for being rude and insubordinate.

The school board scheduled a hearing to decide their punishment. Robert volunteered to be the group's spokesman. He stood before the board members and explained why the students had walked out. The teacher had treated them quite unfairly, he said.

His explanation was convincing. The school board allowed Robert and his friends to return to school. But from then on, the board warned, they had better behave.

Robert Jackson had won his first case.

CHAPTER THREE

"Mark You Jackson"

Robert loved how he felt when he spoke in front of an audience. People kept their eyes on him. They paid attention to what he said. Even though he was only fourteen, he had the power to change their minds.

Robert searched for ways to give more public speeches. He joined the literary society at Frewsburg High School. Every two weeks the group met to debate a subject. When they put on mock trials, Robert played one of the lawyers.

He also signed up for the debate team, which competed with other schools. The teams argued topics such as "Which is most important to the defense of the United States, the army or the navy?"

It appealed to Robert to debate ideas, just as Grandfather Jackson and the other men did at the Frewsburg general store. He liked pulling together arguments in his head. Then he figured out how to present them so that he convinced other people that he was right.

One of the judges at the school debates was impressed by the brown-haired boy in short pants. "He ... was not more than fourteen years old. Holy Moses! You should have heard that boy debate. I was astounded."

Another judge remembered that Robert was "distinctly the best debater in the crowd and we decided the debate in his favor."

Robert received invitations to talk at social gatherings and meetings in Frewsburg and neighboring towns. People enjoyed debates and discussions about history, economics, or politics, and he was an entertaining speaker.

The Woman's Christian Temperance Union regularly invited Robert to speak at their meetings. The WCTU worked to discourage people from drinking alcohol, which members thought created problems for families and communities, such as violence against women and children. The group worked for world peace, better public health, and the involvement of women in politics. At one meeting they asked Robert and a friend to debate whether women should have the right to vote.

Local leaders turned to Robert for special speeches. When he was fifteen, he gave the farewell speech in honor of three retiring teachers at the Frewsburg School. At sixteen, he led a meeting of the county Democratic Party.

Young Orator
In this old family photo, a teenage Robert Jackson dresses up in formal attire and shows off his speaking style.

William Jennings Bryan
(1860–1925) giving a speech during the 1908 Democratic National Convention. Bryan was the Democratic Party's unsuccessful presidential candidate in 1896, 1900, and 1908.

Robert improved his style by listening to experienced speakers. When a candidate for local political office gave a speech in Frewsburg, Robert attended. Sometimes he had the chance to go to lectures at the Chautauqua Institution, an educational center and religious retreat twenty-five miles away. Famous people spoke there, including President Theodore Roosevelt and New York governor Charles Evans Hughes.

In 1907, when he was fifteen, Robert traveled to Chautauqua to hear William Jennings Bryan, one of the most popular orators of the time. A lawyer and Democratic politician, Bryan ran unsuccessfully for U.S. president three times around the beginning of the twentieth century.

Robert later heard Bryan speak several times. He watched the man's hand gestures and facial expressions, and he noticed how Bryan chose his words and varied the tone of his voice. Robert never forgot the way Bryan captivated his audiences with simple language and humor. "I was impressed by his magnetic personality and his oratory ...," Jackson said. "He didn't talk down to the people."

In June 1909, Robert graduated from Frewsburg High School in a class of only three students. As both class president and valedictorian, he gave the graduation oration, called "Labor vs. Capital," about the ongoing conflict between workers and big business. Workers wanted laws to guarantee better pay and shorter hours, while businesses wanted to compete without the government getting in the way. It was the kind of argument about ideas and politics that grabbed Robert's interest.

By now, many of Jackson's friends called him Bob. He was seventeen and had his high school diploma, but he wanted to learn more. Bob decided to study an extra year at the high school in Jamestown, five miles away at the foot of Chautauqua Lake. With a population of thirty-one thousand, Jamestown had a larger school that offered subjects Bob hadn't been able to take in Frewsburg.

Surrounded by rolling farmland, the city was home to several dozen factories that

Jamestown High School, *where Robert Jackson spent an extra year of high school after graduating from Frewsburg High School.*

Defenders of the Cup
The Jamestown High School debate team with the trophy they won in an interscholastic debate. Jackson is seated on the left in this photograph from the Jamestown High School 1910 yearbook.

made wooden and metal furniture and cotton and wool fabrics for clothing. Only the main streets were paved. The roads out of town were dirt.

When school started in September, Bob packed a lunch and jumped on the trolley for the ride from Frewsburg to Jamestown.

He was glad to find that his new school had a debate club, the Lyceum. Every two weeks, the all-male club met to practice debate and public speaking.

Several times a year, the club competed against other schools in formal debates. At one of these debates, Bob and two teammates argued the position that the United States should limit immigration from Europe and Asia. Millions of immigrants had flooded into the country during recent years, most looking for more economic opportunities or religious freedom. The Jamestown team presented the view of many Americans—that immigrants were a burden on society because they lacked job skills and education.

Bob's debating technique improved even more from his practice with the Lyceum. The other members soon recognized his talent. By the second half of the year, they voted him the Lyceum's president.

"He had a style those days that was all his own," one friend remembered. "He would work up his arguments ... and then raise his finger and point and say 'mark you!' To the students he became know[n] as 'Mark You Jackson.'"

Bob was also pleased with the classes and teachers in Jamestown. Early in the year, his English teacher, Mary Willard, asked the class a difficult question. He knew the answer, but he waited for someone to speak up. When no one else volunteered, he raised his hand.

After class, Miss Willard stopped him. "Why, Bob Jackson, where did you learn that?"

He replied that he had read a book on the subject. Miss Willard was impressed that he read so much. After that, she took Bob under her wing. "You must not dare to underestimate your God-given ability," she told him.

At least once a week, Mary Willard invited Jackson to dinner at the house she shared with her sister Vesta. He was grateful for their attention. "They had a fine collection of the best operas and the best music ...," he recalled. "She tried to bring me in contact with the best in literature. ..."

Miss Willard recommended that Bob read William Shakespeare, Charles Dickens, Rudyard Kipling, and dozens of other outstanding authors. She taught him to write about his ideas in a way that readers could easily understand and enjoy.

During the years that followed, Jackson became like a son to Mary Willard. She gave him support and advice, referring to him as her "little Bob." After her death in 1931, he said, "Her influence would be hard to overestimate."

Jackson studied American history and economics with Milton Fletcher, the school's principal. Mr. Fletcher made history come alive, and Bob looked forward to his classes. Years later he said, "I still hope for Mr. Fletcher's approval, still want a passing mark at his hands—and demerits from him would sting as few others could."

Milton Fletcher, *the principal of Jamestown High School from 1899 to 1919. When Fletcher retired as Jamestown school superintendent in 1932, Robert Jackson gave a speech in tribute to him.*

One day Jackson happened to meet his principal on the trolley. They chatted about a violinist who had played a concert in Jamestown the night before. Bob told Mr. Fletcher how amazed he was that the musician had been paid $500 for his performance. "Quite a big fee!" Bob said.

Mr. Fletcher turned to the eighteen-year-old. "You study law ... do as you can with it, and you'll get a $500 fee some day."

That gave Bob something to think about.

In June 1910, Bob Jackson graduated from Jamestown High in a class of

Yearbook Photo
Jackson (standing at the right) and other graduating seniors as they appeared in the Jamestown High School 1910 yearbook.

Robert Jackson,
age eighteen, in his high school graduation photograph. In the Jamestown High School 1910 yearbook, a line appeared under his name: "Mark you! this promising young orator from Frewsburg!"

sixty-two. In his Class Day oration, he spoke about Jamestown's history and natural beauty. At the end of the speech, he said, "Let it be one of the ... tasks of our lives to make this loved home of our youth year by year more worthy of the setting which has been so cunningly fashioned by Nature's matchless handicraft."

Jackson always believed that the schools in Frewsburg and Jamestown gave him "a life-long curiosity for knowledge." To him, learning was "wealth no thief can take away."

Both Mr. Fletcher and Miss Willard encouraged Bob to go into law after he graduated from Jamestown High School. He knew he had a gift for debate and writing—skills a lawyer needed. Two special teachers convinced him that he could do it.

CHAPTER FOUR

Legal Eagle

Bob could imagine himself practicing law. "I hesitate to say that I always intended to be a lawyer," he said, "but that may be true."

His father was set against Bob's becoming a lawyer and refused to pay for law school. William Jackson had a poor opinion of the profession based on some lawyers he'd known.

But Angelina Jackson's cousin offered Bob an apprenticeship in his Jamestown law office. Frank Mott was about twenty years older than Bob and was a leader in the Democratic Party. By working with Mott, Bob could learn about the law firsthand. He jumped at the opportunity, even though he knew it would cause problems at home.

William didn't want his son influenced by a man like Mott, a big spender who was always in debt. William had told Bob many times that a man was dishonorable if he didn't pay people what he owed them. Angelina Jackson liked her cousin, but she didn't take sides.

Bob ignored his father's objections and accepted Frank Mott's offer. He started his apprenticeship in September 1910.

Mott and his partner, Benjamin Dean, taught Bob how to look up answers to legal questions and to prepare cases for court. He read law books and learned how a law practice operated. A year in the office convinced him that law was the profession for him.

Before he could be licensed as a lawyer in New York, Bob had to finish two more years, either in an apprenticeship or in law school. He thought he should

West 3rd St. Jamestown, N. Y.

Jamestown, New York
This postcard shows the city in 1909, the year Jackson traveled by trolley (shown here) from his Frewsburg home to attend Jamestown High School. In 1913, Jackson defended streetcar workers accused of cutting down the poles that held up the trolley wires.

enroll in law school for a year because he hadn't gone to college.

Bob considered schools in New York City, but he couldn't see himself living among several million people. He knew some Jamestown lawyers who had studied at Albany Law School. Albany, New York, had a population of about a hundred thousand. To Bob, it seemed a better fit. He was eager to live in New York's capital, where the state courts and legislature met. He later said, "I thought I would learn more that was not in the books at Albany than in any other place."

Albany Law would award Bob a certificate of graduation after one year of courses. The school's charter didn't allow it to grant him a law degree because he was under age twenty-one. That was fine with Bob. After one more year as an apprentice in Mott's office, he could still take the state's bar exam and become a lawyer.

Because his father wouldn't pay for law school, Bob borrowed the tuition money from his mother's bachelor brother, John Houghwout.

Classes began in the fall of 1911. Bob and two other law students from Jamestown rented an apartment in a three-story building several blocks from the law school. Bob was determined to learn as much as possible during his year in Albany. He studied hard, never missed a single class, and received high grades.

On many afternoons after class, Bob walked across the street to the State Capitol Building. In the courtroom, he watched sessions of the New York State Court of Appeals. To Bob, this was "one of the most important assets of the school." The state's best attorneys argued cases there, and he studied their courtroom style and technique.

Bob took breaks from his long hours of studying by ice-skating on Washington Park Lake, two blocks from his apartment. One winter day while he was skating, a classmate introduced Bob to his cousin, Irene Gerhardt.

Irene was twenty-one and worked as a secretary in the Capitol building. She had grown up in Kingston, New York, sixty miles south of Albany, where her father was a building contractor.

After an afternoon skating together, Bob thought he and Irene had gotten along pretty well. She was attractive and smart. He asked her to skate again, and then to dances. When he graduated from law school in June 1912, he invited Irene to the ceremony.

Bob returned to his apprenticeship in Jamestown, but he and Irene kept up their long-distance relationship. They

William Jackson's New Car
Robert Jackson's parents and sister Helen go for a ride, around 1912. William Jackson owned one of the first cars in Frewsburg. Robert Jackson bought his first car—used—in 1919.

wrote letters, and Bob traveled 350 miles across the state to visit her.

Irene's mother had her doubts about Bob Jackson. She told her daughter, "He's too skinny, and he's never going to amount to anything!" But her comment didn't change Irene's mind.

Frank Mott was glad to have his apprentice back in the office, and he let Bob handle cases as if he were already a lawyer.

Jackson's first trial was the defense of twenty streetcar workers who had been arrested for rioting. The workers had gone on strike, demanding higher pay from the streetcar company. His clients were accused of cutting down poles that held up the trolley wires.

This shut down the electric streetcars, and people in Jamestown were angry with the union. Bob's attorney friends told him that the case would hurt his career. They warned that businessmen wouldn't hire a lawyer who represented unions. Jackson paid no attention to their advice.

The trial was set for September 1913. He had to request special permission from the judge to represent the workers in court because he hadn't taken the bar exam yet.

Bob carefully prepared for the case. People would be watching to see how he performed, and they would remember whether he was a lawyer worth hiring. He put in long hours investigating what had happened the night of the pole cutting. He talked to everybody involved and studied the laws about riots and conspiracy.

As he expected, the local newspaper reporters showed up in court. During the trial, Jackson questioned the prosecution's witnesses who had pointed the finger at his clients. He revealed that these men had helped cut down the poles. The judge threw out the case against Jackson's clients because the prosecution's only witnesses were accomplices in the crime.

Jackson said later that from then "until the day I quit practicing law my office was always full of business." In years to come, he would represent other unions. Businessmen hired him anyway because he won his cases.

Franklin Delano Roosevelt (1882–1945) in 1913 when he was assistant secretary of the Navy under President Woodrow Wilson. During this period, FDR helped Jackson and Frank Mott arrange political appointments in the Jamestown area.

By November 1913, Bob had passed the bar exam and could practice law in New York State. He knew he had more to learn, though. He spent time with Jamestown's lawyers, listening to them discuss cases and trials. "You absorbed a great deal by association with those experienced, older men," he said.

While Jackson was preparing for his legal career, Frank Mott pulled him into Democratic Party politics. In 1911, Mott introduced him to Franklin Delano Roosevelt, a first-term state senator from the eastern part of New York.

Jackson and FDR
Robert Jackson and Frank Mott had a longtime political relationship with Franklin Roosevelt. In this July 13, 1929, photograph, Frank Mott hosts Governor Roosevelt during his visit to Chautauqua County when FDR gave a speech at the Chautauqua Institution. In the backseat are FDR (with the hat) and Frank Mott. Robert Jackson stands beside Mott. The younger man standing near the front of the car is FDR's son Elliott.

Jackson watched Roosevelt in his skirmishes with state politicians. "Politically, he was all amateur. ... He was like a hothouse plant just set out among weathered and hardy rivals." Yet Roosevelt's charm helped him win battles.

With Mott's help, Jackson was elected to the Democratic Party's state committee in 1913. He was only twenty-one. One of his responsibilities was to reward Democratic supporters with jobs, such as the local postmaster position. By then, Franklin Roosevelt was assistant secretary of the Navy in the administration of President Woodrow Wilson, a Democrat. Roosevelt used his influence in Washington to help Jackson arrange these patronage appointments.

But Bob disliked the party infighting and people constantly asking him for political jobs. It took too much time away from his law practice. From then on, he vowed to stay out of political organizing.

Jackson continued to support Democratic candidates and to give speeches on their behalf, although he never ran for office. He didn't think he had a chance in Republican-voting Jamestown. "It was great good fortune for me to be so far in the minority," he said later, "that I couldn't ... be elected member of the [New York State] Assembly or some local political office."

In 1914, as Jackson started his career, Great Britain, France, and Russia were

World War I
(1914–1918). A British Red Cross orderly helps a captured wounded German soldier to a field hospital in France.

Irene Gerhardt Jackson
(1890–1986). This portrait is from 1928, when Irene was thirty-eight. An active horsewoman and volunteer for charitable organizations, Irene once told a reporter that her role in her husband's career was to make things run smoothly at home so that he didn't have to worry about those matters.

battling against Germany, Austria-Hungary, and the Ottoman Empire. Bob supported President Wilson, who wanted to keep America out of this great world war.

Bob's family had always been against wars, and none of them had fought in one since the American Revolution. His years of reading American and world history had made Bob cautious about war. He didn't think that it ever really settled problems and, instead, often destroyed the countries that fought.

By this time, Bob had earned enough from practicing law to pay back his uncle for the law-school loan. His father admitted that Bob had done well and was proud when people complimented his son's legal work.

Yet Bob felt that their relationship wasn't the same: "In his later life he marred ... his relations with me to some extent, by drinking rather heavily." In January 1915, William Jackson died from a heart condition and alcoholism.

After his father's death, Bob took responsibility for his family in Frewsburg. He became guardian of his eleven-year-old sister, Helen, and along with sister Ella he helped their mother when she needed it.

Now that Bob had established his law practice, he could support a wife. He bought a newly built, two-story house in Jamestown within walking distance of his office. He set up one of the spare bedrooms to use as a library when he brought work home at night. The backyard had space for a vegetable garden.

In April 1916, Bob and Irene were married after four years of dating. They had a wedding in Albany for close friends and family. Frank Mott was Bob's best man, and Irene's sister Elizabeth was her bridesmaid. For their honeymoon, the couple traveled to Virginia and Washington, D.C.

One year later in April 1917, the United States entered the Great War, later called World War I. Although other men were drafted to serve in the army, Bob wasn't called because he was the main support of his wife.

War Controversy
President Woodrow Wilson (far left) and his secretary of state, William Jennings Bryan, in 1913. Bryan resigned his position in 1915 to protest Wilson's handling of the sinking of the ocean liner Lusitania *by a German submarine, which killed nearly twelve hundred people. Bryan wanted the United States to stay neutral after the outbreak of World War I. The sinking outraged Americans and helped pull the country into the war against Germany two years later.*

Woodrow Wilson *(1856– 1924) in 1912, the year he was elected president.*

Most people in Jamestown were in favor of the United States' sending troops to help the European Allies. Bob thought the war was a mistake, and he was disappointed when President Wilson changed his mind and got the country involved.

Bob Jackson had his own ideas and he stuck to them, no matter what others said. In his office, he kept a framed quotation by British author Rudyard Kipling that summed up Jackson's independence: "He travels fastest who travels alone."

Jackson never felt that his views hurt his law practice. When people needed a good lawyer, they didn't care about his politics. Bob had many friends who disagreed with his politics, too. One said of him, "He never yielded his convictions, but in his personal association he was singularly tolerant of the views of other people."

Gradually, Bob built up his list of clients. He fought legal battles for businesses such as local telephone companies, railroads, and banks, as well as for the city of Jamestown. He also represented individual people, small businessmen, and farmers.

"I like the combat," he once said. "When I see six fellows on one side and two on the other, I always feel like joining the two. ... I was never a crusader. I just liked a good fight!"

In one case, a farmer came to Jackson because he'd been tricked when buying a pregnant Holstein cow. The seller claimed the cow had been bred with a Holstein bull, so the farmer had paid extra to get the Holstein calf. He knew he'd been cheated when the newborn calf turned out to be a Jersey.

Jackson sued the seller on the farmer's behalf. "We tried the love life of the bossie cow with the whole community attending," Jackson recalled. He won the case, and his client received the fifteen dollars he'd wanted. Jackson's payment was five dollars.

No matter how small the case, Bob gave each client his best. "I tried to anticipate every possible move an adversary could make and have my mind ready as to how I would meet whatever he did."

A lawyer who knew him said, "I should hate to tell of the times he outwitted me. ... He never neglected the most painstaking preparation."

At five feet nine inches tall, Jackson didn't look like a powerful man in the courtroom. But according to one of his law partners, he "had a powerful effect on the juries." When Jackson summed up his case, it was as if he were having a private conversation with the jury.

Another Jamestown attorney believed Jackson's knack for reading people helped him win cases. He could "tune in quickly on a person and perceive exactly what kind of person he was."

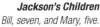

Jackson's Children
Bill, seven, and Mary, five.

By 1919 the war in Europe had ended. In July, Bob and Irene had their first child, William Eldred. After daughter Mary Margaret was born in 1921, the family moved into a large old house just outside the city. Bob had enough land to build a stable and keep a couple of horses. There was room for his garden and a sandbox for the children.

Bob tried to be with Bill and Mary as much as possible as they were growing up. He closed his office on Saturdays so that he could be home all weekend, even though most Jamestown lawyers stayed open that day.

Mary shared her father's passion for horses, and they often went riding together on weekends. In the summers, the two camped and rode on the old family farm in Pennsylvania.

Bill liked music and played piano and organ. He practiced on the organ at St. Luke's Episcopal Church, where the family attended, and he sometimes played for the church service. When Bill got older, Bob encouraged his son's interest in law. He took the boy to court and had him run errands in the law office.

Going for a Ride
The Jacksons with their horses and dog, in the late 1920s. From left: Mary on Buster, Bill on Gray Goose, Irene on Blue Bonnet, and Bob Jackson on Augusta.

Together, the family fished, hunted, skated, and rode horses—the same outdoor activities Bob had loved as a boy. He bought a thirty-foot boat, *The Alibi*, and took family and friends out on Chautauqua Lake.

When he relaxed, Bob avoided anything that required scorekeeping, such as golf and bridge. "Since my work is a continuous round of contest and competition," he once said, "I prefer only hobbies which are non-competitive."

In October 1929, the stock market crashed. Soon the United States plunged into the Great Depression. In Jamestown and in the rest of the country, banks failed and factories closed. Jobs disappeared and prices for farmers' crops fell. People who owed money lost everything when their debts were called in and they couldn't pay.

Destitute Man
An unemployed man leans against a vacant store in 1935. During the Great Depression, businesses closed down, putting people out of work. Photojournalist Dorothea Lange (1895–1965) took many photographs like this one for the Farm Security Administration. Her work documented the widespread poverty during the Depression, particularly among farm workers.

Bob wrote to his former teacher Mary Willard and her sister Vesta after they moved to California. He told them that property wasn't selling and that the furniture businesses and banks in Jamestown had suffered.

Jackson was lucky. His law practice remained successful. Even during the early 1930s when one in four people had no job, he was making $30,000 a year, equal to nearly $500,000 today.

Bob could afford to take his family on winter vacations to Florida, Cuba, Bermuda, Arizona, and California. He and Irene were also able to buy, with two other couples, a farm outside of Jamestown where they raised horses.

As the Depression continued, people became frustrated that President Herbert Hoover, a Republican, hadn't done enough to solve their economic problems. The 1932 presidential election focused on the Depression.

Franklin Roosevelt was the Democratic Party's candidate. During the twenty years since Bob had first met him, Roosevelt had risen from the New York State Senate to become governor in 1929. Bob had helped with his campaigns and worked with him on government projects such as a state commission that studied crime and the justice system.

Bob liked Roosevelt. Yet when the Democratic Party nominated him for president, Jackson wrote to Vesta Willard, "I can't say Roosevelt was my choice or that I can get very much enthused about him. He is a fine man but not very heavy."

Still, Jackson campaigned for Roosevelt that fall. Franklin Roosevelt promised to give Americans a "New Deal" that would end the Depression. The voters liked what he said, and in the November election Roosevelt defeated President Hoover.

Less than two years later, Bob Jackson would find himself in Washington helping Franklin Roosevelt with his New Deal program.

A New Administration
Franklin Roosevelt (right) and Herbert Hoover (1874–1964) ride to the U.S. Capitol for Roosevelt's inauguration on March 4, 1933. FDR defeated President Hoover in the November 1932 election.

CHAPTER FIVE

New Deal Lawyer

Bob Jackson was impressed by what Franklin Delano Roosevelt accomplished in his first three months as president. FDR convinced Congress to pass laws that created jobs, helped the bankrupt farmers, and rescued failing small businesses.

Jackson had grown up in a community where people took care of themselves, but he saw how hard the Depression hit. He agreed with Roosevelt that the federal government had to step in to put the country back on its feet.

Before long, Jackson received calls from New York Democrats who had gone to Washington with Roosevelt. Jackson was a faithful Democrat and a leading lawyer in western New York, they said. The Roosevelt administration could use him.

At first Jackson politely refused. He was flattered, but none of the government positions they offered seemed right for him. Besides, he liked practicing law in Jamestown. Bob had lived in the area most of his life, and his closest friends were there. So were his mother, his sisters and their families, and other relatives he'd known since his boyhood days.

"Migrant Mother"
An unemployed migrant worker in California sits under a tent with some of her seven children. This famous 1936 photograph by photojournalist Dorothea Lange became a symbol of the Depression.

Then in the fall of 1933, Jackson heard from Acting Secretary of the Treasury Henry Morgenthau, Jr., whom he knew through New York Democratic Party politics. Secretary Morgenthau was looking for a lawyer to try cases against people who owed taxes to the government. He offered Jackson the job as general counsel for the Treasury Department's Bureau of Revenue.

Jackson considered the offer. The legal work sounded challenging and interesting. It might be his chance to help with the New Deal. Some of Jackson's friends thought the experience in Washington would be good for his career, while others advised him to stay out of the politics there.

Irene was willing to move. She was happy in Jamestown, but she didn't have the ties to it that Bob did. Bob knew that she was less outgoing than he was, though. Making friends in a new place would be harder for her.

One thing made the decision easier. If the family moved to Washington, they'd be close to Bill, who had started high school there in September. Jamestown High School was running on half-day sessions while a new building was under construction. Bob and Irene didn't think that schedule was good for Bill's education. Instead, they had chosen St. Albans School, a private school in Washington.

Bob decided to take the job at Treasury—on a trial basis for six months. He was eager to see what he could do in Washington. Jackson told Secretary Morgenthau that he wanted to spend just four days a week in Washington. On weekends, he would travel the three hundred miles back to Jamestown. He planned to keep his law practice going in case he changed his mind about the Treasury job. Secretary Morgenthau agreed.

In February 1934, Jackson started work at the Bureau of Revenue. He was in charge of about three hundred lawyers who argued their cases to a Board of Tax Appeals. Jackson had never managed that many people, and he had to learn how to deal with the government bureaucracy.

It was a big change living in Washington, a city with a population of about a half million. In Jamestown Bob knew the people he passed on the street. He was used to a spacious house with his garden and his horses. He could take out his boat on the lake when he felt like it. Now the Jackson family lived in an apartment in the Wardman Park Hotel. Both children, who had always gone to public school, attended private schools near the apartment.

Once he settled in, Jackson liked the job. But he soon realized the work was too time-consuming for him to commute back to New York State on weekends. He shut down his Jamestown law practice and committed himself to the New Deal.

Jackson was too busy to take off on weekends or to go on winter vacations with the family. During the summer, Irene and the children returned to Jamestown, but Bob had to stay in Washington to work. He was able to make only short trips to visit his mother and sisters in Frewsburg.

Not long after Jackson arrived at the Treasury Department, a well-publicized case landed on his desk. The Justice Department asked his office to prosecute Andrew Mellon for evading income taxes.

Mellon was one of the richest men in America, having made a fortune in banking and industry. From 1921 through 1932, Mellon had been the Secretary of the Treasury under presidents Harding, Coolidge, and Hoover, all Republicans.

After Jackson studied the facts of the case, he agreed that Andrew Mellon owed taxes. But he recommended against charging Mellon with intentional tax fraud because fraud was hard to prove. The Justice Department and President Roosevelt overruled his advice.

To Jackson, their decision seemed political. Many people blamed Mellon and the Hoover administration for the Depression. The tax case was a way for Democrats to get even with the Republicans.

Secretary Morgenthau told Jackson, "I consider that Mr. Mellon is not on trial but democracy and the privileged rich [are] and I want to see who will win."

Robert Jackson was looking for a challenge when he came to Washington. Now he had it. To prove that Andrew Mellon evaded taxes, he had to collect and study piles of complicated evidence about Mellon's business dealings.

Harding and Mellon
In this 1922 photograph, President Warren Harding (1865–1923) (left) buys three treasury savings certificates from Treasury Secretary Andrew Mellon (1855–1937). From 1921 to 1932, Mellon was treasury secretary for three Republican presidents, Harding, Coolidge, and Hoover.

Andrew Mellon hired one of the nation's top lawyers, Frank Hogan, to defend him. Hogan's strategy was to gain sympathy for Andrew Mellon from the Board of Tax Appeals—and the press. In April 1935, he put his elderly client on the stand to testify.

Jackson had twenty years of experience questioning witnesses. He had to be careful when he cross-examined the eighty-year-old Mellon. If Jackson was too aggressive, he would play into Hogan's hands.

Smiling, Jackson approached the white-haired man sitting behind the rails of the witness chair. At first he was friendly. He let Andrew Mellon ramble as he answered questions about his business.

Then Jackson changed his tone. In a firm voice, he asked Mellon about a stock-sale deal designed to reduce his income taxes. Mellon denied selling the stock for that reason.

Are you absolutely sure? Jackson asked him. Mellon insisted he was.

Reaching for the stack of documents on his table, Jackson snatched out a paper. It was evidence showing that Mellon had schemed to avoid paying taxes.

Mellon pushed up his glasses and studied the paper. His hands trembled. With the evidence in front of him, he had to admit he had made certain business deals to evade taxes.

Again and again that day, Jackson forced Andrew Mellon to admit using tax-dodging tricks.

Because of Mellon's fame, Bob Jackson was in the national spotlight. He was no longer just a country lawyer from upstate New York, unknown to most Americans.

The Mellon tax hearings continued on and off for a year and a half. Finally in December 1937, the Board of Tax Appeals ruled that Andrew Mellon owed the U.S. government more than $600,000 in taxes, but it did not find him guilty of fraud. Jackson was satisfied with the board's decision. He knew from the start that fraud would be hard to prove.

Andrew Mellon never learned that he'd been cleared of fraud. He died of cancer four months before the board announced its decision.

In the fall of 1935, as the Mellon case dragged on, Jackson went to Europe to investigate another tax case against an international company. When he was in Germany, he saw Nazi storm troopers everywhere he went. "I had a feeling ... that things were not right," Jackson said. "Germany was a danger spot to me from then on."

The year before, Adolf Hitler had become dictator of Germany by crushing his political opposition. He began to build up the country's military in violation of the Treaty of Versailles, the peace agreement reached after Germany's defeat by the Allies in World War I. Other European countries nervously watched Germany's actions.

After Italy invaded Ethiopia in 1935, Europe looked even more turbulent. The U.S. Congress passed the first of several Neutrality Acts to make sure that the country did not get involved in any foreign conflicts as it had during World War I.

The Rise of Hitler
After his 1935 trip to Germany, Jackson was uneasy about Adolf Hitler's rise to power. Accompanied by two of his generals, Hitler (1889–1945) salutes the crowd at the 1937 Nazi Party Day in Nuremberg, Germany.

Later in 1935, Jackson returned to Jamestown to speak at the dedication of the new Jamestown High School building. What he had seen in Europe was on his mind. "After a 'war to end war,' we find Europe seething with militarism again and only waiting some dramatic collision of lawless forces to break into strife again."

After two years in Washington, Robert Jackson had made a name for himself. *Time* magazine called him "one of the nation's ablest trial lawyers." He was known for his skillful oratory and the elegant way he dressed—the three-piece suit and the perfectly folded handkerchief in his breast pocket.

Jackson felt he was different from others who had come to work on Roosevelt's New Deal. At forty-four, he was older than most of the bright, well-

On The Alibi
Robert Jackson takes his family out on Chautauqua Lake in his boat, around 1937. Jackson loved outdoor activities. Behind Jackson (left to right): nephew Harold Adams (not pictured); wife Irene; sister Ella Jackson Springer; mother Angelina; and sister Helen Jackson Adams.

educated New Dealers from Ivy League law schools. "I wasn't a member of the so-called 'brain trust,'" he said. "I never even went to college. ... I never had served in the political national committee, ran for office, had a political following. ... I was pretty much outside of all those groups and yet friendly with many of the members of all of them."

Bob Jackson's legal skills impressed the brain trust. One Harvard-educated lawyer who worked with him commented later, "Jackson had a first-rate, incisive mind, an eloquent pen, and a belligerently liberal faith."

In early 1936, Jackson's abilities and New York connection to President Roosevelt earned him another promotion—assistant attorney general in the Justice Department's Tax Division. The new position gave Jackson more trial experience as he handled tax cases in courts throughout the country, including the Supreme Court.

That November, Franklin Roosevelt was reelected to a second term. Jackson had been thinking about going back to private law practice in Jamestown after the election. Then Attorney General Homer Cummings offered to make him head of the Antitrust Division of the Justice Department.

The lawyers in this division prosecuted businesses that broke antitrust laws. These laws had been written to prevent monopolies, in which one company becomes so large that it shuts out competition.

As a lawyer in Jamestown, Bob Jackson had seen small companies squeezed

THE SUPREME COURT

The Supreme Court is the highest court in the United States.

The U.S. Congress sets the number of justices who sit on the Court. Since 1869, the Supreme Court has included one chief justice and eight associate justices. The president nominates the justices to a lifetime term. The Senate must approve each appointment.

The U.S. Constitution doesn't specifically describe the Supreme Court's powers. In 1803 under the fourth chief justice, John Marshall, the Court staked out its power. From that time on, the Supreme Court has decided whether the actions of the president, Congress, or states are allowed by the Constitution. This is called judicial review. For more than two hundred years, the Court has interpreted the meaning of the Constitution in different ways.

Most Supreme Court cases begin in a state or federal court. The losing side of a legal dispute has the right to ask an appeals court to reconsider the case. If the loser of the appeal isn't satisfied with that court's decision, it may ask the Supreme Court to look at the case.

Each case is given a name, such as *Brown v. Board of Education of Topeka*. The first part (*Brown*) is the side that lost in the lower court and then asked the Supreme Court to review the case. The *v* stands for *versus*. The last part (*Board of Education of Topeka*) is the opposing side that won in the lower court.

The justices choose which cases they will review during the Court term. The term starts the first Monday in October and ends in June. Four of the nine justices must vote to take a case. When the Court turns down a case, the lower court's decision stands.

During Robert Jackson's last term as a justice in 1953–1954, the Supreme Court received about fourteen hundred requests. Today the Court gets nearly ten thousand cases each year and accepts fewer than one hundred. Law clerks help the justices review the requests and do legal research.

After the Supreme Court agrees to hear a case, lawyers from both sides file briefs with the Court. In a brief, lawyers explain why they think the law supports their side.

Next, the nine justices listen to the lawyers' oral arguments in the courtroom. Each side has thirty minutes to convince the justices of its viewpoint. The justices interrupt the lawyers to ask questions. There are no witnesses and no jury.

After the oral arguments, the justices vote in a private conference. The majority decides how the Court will rule on the case.

If the chief justice agrees with the majority, he assigns one of the justices to write the Court's opinion. The opinion explains the reasons for the Court's decision. When the chief is on the minority side, the most senior justice on the majority side assigns the opinion.

Any justice is free to write a separate opinion either agreeing (concurring) or disagreeing (dissenting) with the Court's decision.

Months may pass before the written opinions about a case are finished and the justices are ready to announce the Court's majority decision. Each justice who wrote an opinion may read it in the courtroom.

The Supreme Court's ruling on a case is the final word.

out of business by bigger ones. "I thought society was better off if business was not allowed to get too big," he said. He accepted the job in January 1937.

Assistant Attorney General Jackson traveled around the country making speeches about why it was important to enforce antitrust laws. Monopolies put too much power and wealth in the hands of a few people, he told his audiences. Jackson blamed these big companies for slowing down the economy's recovery from the Depression.

New Dealers admired his attacks on big business. Secretary of the Interior Harold Ickes wrote in his diary that Jackson "is the kind of man we need in our public life if we are to escape disaster."

President Roosevelt hadn't publicly taken a stand against monopolies, but he let Jackson know he was glad he had made the speeches. FDR encouraged him to give more of them.

The national newspapers often covered Jackson's speeches. Some people didn't like his criticism of business. Bob Jackson gained a reputation for being one of the most liberal—even radical—members of the Roosevelt administration.

Opponents of the New Deal accused the federal government of taking too much power. Lawsuits reached the Supreme Court, charging that the Constitution did not allow Congress to make laws controlling private business.

The Supreme Court agreed. By majority vote, the Court struck down ten New Deal laws within two years. Never had a Supreme Court overturned so many laws in such a short period. These laws had given workers the right to form unions, had set wages and prices, and had stopped unfair business competition.

In Jackson's opinion, the Court was dead wrong. He saw nothing in the Constitution that stopped Congress from passing these laws. The country needed the New Deal legislation to recover from the Depression, and the Supreme Court was standing in the way. In a speech, Jackson said, "The Court ... refuses to see the real and living problems which men are trying to solve. ..."

President Roosevelt was worried that the Supreme Court might undo his entire New Deal program. He'd been unable to appoint any new justices who supported his views, because none of the nine justices had died or retired.

Roosevelt's landslide reelection in 1936 convinced him that voters approved of the New Deal. He assumed he had the support of Congress and the public to do something about the Court.

In February 1937, FDR announced that the Supreme Court was backlogged with cases because the justices were too old to keep up. He argued that Congress had changed the number of Supreme Court justices six times since 1789. It was time to do it again.

Roosevelt asked Congress to pass a new law: If a federal judge didn't retire by age seventy, the president could appoint an additional judge to the court.

Six of the Supreme Court justices were over seventy. The law would allow Roosevelt to make six new appointments.

Bob Jackson was on a train coming back to Washington from New York when he first read about Roosevelt's court-packing plan in a newspaper. He was in favor of change on the Court, but this plan wasn't the best way. Only a few people knew about it beforehand. Roosevelt hadn't informed leaders in Congress, and they didn't like new bills sprung on them.

Court-Packing Testimony
On March 11, 1937, Assistant Attorney General Jackson testified before the Senate Judiciary Committee about President Roosevelt's court-packing proposal. In his statement, Jackson told senators that Congress had the power to change the size of the Supreme Court—and should use it.

Jackson visited Jamestown a couple of weeks later. He spoke to friends and family, who didn't approve of the president's personal attacks on the Supreme Court justices.

Back in Washington, Jackson told FDR that his court-packing bill was in trouble. "This thing has got to be put in different terms or you're going to lose the country." He advised the president to talk about the justices' anti–New Deal decisions, not their ages.

In March, the Senate Judiciary Committee called Assistant Attorney General Jackson to testify about the court-packing bill. Reporters and spectators crowded into the Senate Caucus Room for the hearing.

Jackson explained that when the Supreme Court struck down New Deal laws, it took away Congress's

Herbert Hoover and Charles Evans Hughes
At the time of this 1924 photograph, the future president Hoover (left) and future Supreme Court chief justice Hughes (1862–1948) were members of President Calvin Coolidge's cabinet. Hoover was secretary of commerce, and Hughes was secretary of state. In 1929, Hoover succeeded Coolidge as president and appointed Hughes as chief justice, a position he held from 1930 to 1941.

role as the lawmaking branch of government. The voters wanted their elected representatives to pass these laws. "There is a serious lag between public opinion and the decisions of the Court," he told the senators.

Time magazine reported on the hearing. "Honest 'Bob' Jackson made out a case for the President's plan which earned the praise of its bitterest foes, delighted its friends as perhaps the most persuasive yet presented."

Despite the praise, Jackson was afraid his words weren't going to change anyone's mind.

Supreme Court Chief Justice Charles Evans Hughes sent a letter to the Senate denying that the Supreme Court was behind in its cases. After that, both Republicans and Democrats in Congress turned against FDR's court-packing bill. The bill didn't get enough support to pass through Congress, and the number of Supreme Court justices stayed at nine.

Later that spring, FDR got what he wanted anyway. In new cases that came before the Supreme Court, more of the justices voted to support New Deal laws. The majority view had shifted, and the Court allowed the laws to stand.

Then in the summer of 1937, the older justices began to retire. Now FDR had a chance to replace them with justices who agreed with his views. These changes on the Court would eventually affect Robert Jackson's future.

CHAPTER SIX

Ambitions and Promises

By fall of 1937, Jackson was frustrated. Too much of his time was swallowed up by political issues. He wanted to do legal work. That was why he had come to Washington. It was what he was most qualified to do.

Jackson made an appointment to see the president. Roosevelt, who often had early morning meetings in his pajamas, was eating breakfast in bed.

Taking the chair by FDR's bedside, Jackson told the president that he planned to resign as assistant attorney general and return to his law practice. It was expensive to live in Washington and keep his house in Jamestown. Soon he'd have to pay college tuition for both Bill and Mary.

"Bob, you can't leave now," said Roosevelt. "You're in this thing. You can't quit. ..." FDR had plans for Jackson. "If you can be elected governor in '38, you would be in an excellent position for the Presidency in 1940. I don't intend to run."

Jackson wasn't sure he wanted to run for governor of New York—or for president. "I told the President that I did not think my capacities lay in the direction of political office," he later wrote. "I had been fairly successful as a lawyer and preferred to stick to the law."

FDR made another offer. He expected changes in the Justice Department. Jackson should wait a little longer.

Bob Jackson didn't know exactly what the president was promising, but it sounded like a promotion. He agreed to stay in Washington, at least for a while.

Later in 1937, Jackson realized that Roosevelt still intended to push him for governor of New York. FDR invited Jackson on a fishing trip with other close friends and aides. Many Roosevelt watchers, including the press and politicians,

Going Fishing
In late November 1937, President Roosevelt invited Jackson on a fishing trip in Florida with his closest aides. Standing from left to right are military aide Colonel Edwin "Pa" Watson, naval aide Captain Walter Woodson, Assistant Attorney General Jackson, Harry Hopkins (political adviser and head of the Works Progress Administration), and Dr. Ross McIntire (FDR's personal doctor). Seated are FDR and Secretary of the Interior Harold Ickes.

considered this a sign that Roosevelt favored Jackson to eventually succeed him in the White House.

New York's Democratic politicians didn't share Roosevelt's enthusiasm for Bob Jackson. They thought Jackson's antimonopoly speeches showed he was too radical to run for governor of New York, a probusiness state. A few of the Democratic Party leaders had their own ambitions to be governor or president. Others had lost political battles with Roosevelt and were eager to get even with him by blocking Jackson's candidacy.

Despite help from Roosevelt, Jackson couldn't win enough support from New York's Democratic leaders to run for governor. Later he said, "It [the governorship] wasn't anything that I had set my heart on having. I can't say that there ever was a moment of real disappointment about it."

Roosevelt's friends wished Jackson had fought harder to become governor. One said that he wasn't "born for roughhouse combat."

Tom Corcoran, a close FDR adviser, commented that Jackson's "one fault is that he is too likely to become discouraged. He has not yet learned to stand up under fire directed at him personally. ..."

Secretary of the Interior Harold Ickes discussed Jackson's possible presidential candidacy with Roosevelt. "I said that Bob Jackson had the character and the social outlook that would make him an acceptable liberal candidate," Ickes later wrote, "but the President doubted whether he had sufficient political experience."

Despite what had happened with the New York governor's race, Roosevelt kept Jackson close. He included Jackson in his Kitchen Cabinet, a group of trusted men who advised the president. A *Washington Post* column called Jackson "the best spokesman for the New Deal policies and in many ways the best all-around man in the Roosevelt circle."

Chatting with the President's Mother
Assistant Attorney General Jackson talks with President Roosevelt's mother, Sara, at a New York State Democratic Party dinner, January 1938. At this time, FDR was grooming Jackson for a run as New York governor.

FDR invited Jackson to regular poker games. The games were friendly, and by the end of the night, only a few dollars changed hands. These evenings with friends helped the president take his mind off work. Jackson enjoyed joking and relaxing with the group.

Four months after Jackson had threatened to resign, FDR kept his promise of a promotion in the Department of Justice. In March 1938, the president appointed him to the position of solicitor general, the official in charge of arguing the government's side of cases before the Supreme Court. It was the kind of trial work that Jackson loved.

"The only office I ever really coveted was that of Solicitor General of the United States," Jackson later wrote. "It had seemed so far out of reach of a country lawyer ... that I never entertained the thought seriously of occupying the place."

In its March 1938 issue, *Fortune* magazine reported that Jackson had the "brains, nerve, and a persuasive tongue" for the job.

Robert Jackson never forgot the first time he appeared as solicitor general

Courtroom of the U.S. Supreme Court
The room has marble walls and a forty-four-foot ceiling. The nine justices sit behind a mahogany bench in front of the red velvet curtain and four marble columns.

before the Supreme Court. The nine Supreme Court justices sat behind the raised mahogany bench at the front of the Court Chamber. A red velvet curtain and four majestic marble columns rose behind them. On the upper walls surrounding the courtroom, marble panels highlighted the history of law.

He approached the lectern. Adjusting his pince-nez, he looked up at the nine men in black robes. As Jackson made his argument before the Court, he used the same techniques that he had developed as a lawyer in Jamestown. He didn't write out his argument beforehand, but spoke instead from a well-prepared outline and notes.

Jackson was an expert at cutting to the heart of a case with his persuasive arguments. Justice Louis Brandeis once said, "Jackson should be Solicitor General for life."

As solicitor general, Jackson successfully defended several New Deal laws before the Supreme Court, including those dealing with bankruptcy, taxes, and farm programs. He was modest about his performances, later joking to a group of lawyers. "I made three arguments of every case. First came the one that I planned—as I thought, logical, coherent, complete. Second was the one actually presented—interrupted, incoherent, disjointed, disappointing. The third was the utterly devastating argument that I thought of after going to bed that night."

One of his assistant solicitors said Robert Jackson was "supremely confident of himself and his judgment. He had a calm which no crisis could disturb, and standards of honorable conduct which were both rigorous and unshakeable."

Near the end of his career, Jackson called his time as solicitor general "the most enjoyable period of my whole official life." But Roosevelt fueled Jackson's ambitions by talking of a possible presidential candidacy and a seat on the Supreme Court.

In February 1939, Justice Brandeis retired from the Supreme Court. Jackson heard the rumors that FDR was going to appoint him to the Court. For a lawyer, there was no greater honor.

Cutting a Few Figures
Bob and Irene Jackson go ice-skating in Washington, February 1939. Twenty-seven years before, the couple skated together on their first date.

FDR called Jackson into his White House office. The president's news was a letdown. The Supreme Court position would go to William Douglas, another member of FDR's Kitchen Cabinet.

Roosevelt told Jackson that he needed his help in the cabinet. As soon as he could shuffle around a few people, he'd bring Bob in as attorney general. FDR hinted that eventually he would appoint Jackson to the Supreme Court, but for now, the president wanted him to stay as solicitor general.

Jackson's friends could see he was upset. Harold Ickes wrote in his diary: "Bob Jackson ... stayed on as Solicitor General ... on the distinct promise from the President that within a short time ... Jackson would be appointed Attorney General. ... Bob is threatening to resign."

Jackson didn't quit. During that summer while the Supreme Court was in recess, he had a break from his solicitor general duties and could get away from Washington and its politics. He, Irene, and Mary drove across the country, stopping at ranches to ride horses.

While they traveled, Jackson paid attention to the news from Europe. His son, Bill, was touring there with college friends, and Jackson was concerned.

Justices at the White House
In October 1939, the Supreme Court justices paid a visit to President Roosevelt. Solicitor General Robert H. Jackson stands at the left. From left to right: Justices Felix Frankfurter and Hugo Black; a court reporter; Justice Harlan Stone; Chief Justice Charles Evans Hughes; Justices Owen J. Roberts, Stanley Reed, and William Douglas; and Attorney General Frank Murphy. FDR would later appoint both Murphy and Jackson to the Court, in 1940 and 1941 respectively. (Justices James McReynolds and Pierce Butler were absent.)

During the past three years, Germany's leader, Adolf Hitler, had broken several treaties and had taken over Austria and Czechoslovakia. Jackson didn't expect Hitler to stop with those countries. The German military buildup and aggression were signs that Hitler planned to take over all of eastern Europe.

By the end of the summer of 1939, Bill was safe in London and ready to sail home. Jackson drove to Jamestown to visit his mother for the Labor Day weekend. She had not been well, and Bob's sisters had been looking after her.

While he was there, Jackson got an urgent phone call from the White House. Could he come back to Washington right away? The situation in Europe was serious and the president might need his legal advice.

The next day Jackson drove to Washington. The evening was warm and starlit when he arrived at the White House. Roosevelt had invited a few close friends and aides for dinner and poker. The president said he wanted to forget about the world's problems for one evening.

The day before, September 1, 1939, the German army had invaded Poland. Great Britain and France demanded that Hitler withdraw or they would declare war on Germany.

Throughout the evening, Jackson and the others played poker with the president in his study. Aides occasionally brought FDR messages from Europe. Around ten o'clock, Roosevelt read the latest one and then looked around the table at his friends. "Gentlemen, by noon tomorrow, war will have been declared," he said solemnly.

World War II had begun.

The next night Roosevelt gave a radio address. He assured the nation that the United States would stay out of the conflict, even though Great Britain and France had declared war on Germany. It was what most Americans hoped to hear. They assumed the oceans would protect them from the troubles elsewhere.

Jackson had doubts that America could stay neutral for long, especially if Britain and France didn't hold off Hitler's army. He wondered "how long we could stand by and see the last bastions of Western civilization wiped out."

Over the next several months, Britain and France trained soldiers and prepared to battle Hitler. President Roosevelt stuck by his plan to keep the United States neutral, but he began to prepare the country's military for war in case the worst happened.

In November, Supreme Court Justice Pierce Butler died. Roosevelt appointed Attorney General Frank Murphy to the Court and, as he had promised, promoted Jackson to the cabinet as attorney general.

To honor him, his Jamestown friends organized a dinner for Jackson at the Hotel Jamestown. More than eight hundred family, friends, and neighbors came to celebrate his appointment—the largest banquet that Jamestown had ever had.

On January 18, 1940, Robert Jackson took his oath as attorney general. "Thus I stepped out of the office in the executive branch . . . that I had enjoyed most and into a sea of troubles," he later wrote.

As attorney general in FDR's cabinet, Jackson served as head of the Department of Justice. He was the chief legal adviser to the president and to the rest of the executive branch. He was responsible

Celebrating
Irene and Bob dress up for a White House reception in January 1940. Jackson had just been nominated to the attorney general position.

for hundreds of people, including the government's lawyers, the FBI, and the Immigration Service.

President Roosevelt often called Jackson to the White House to discuss problems at the end of the day or at a bedroom breakfast meeting. "You might say that Roosevelt was never closed for business," Jackson said.

Roosevelt had his hands full. That spring Hitler's army swept across Europe, occupying Denmark, Norway, Holland, and Belgium. In June 1940, France surrendered to the Germans. Everyone had expected France to put up more of a fight. Jackson realized that the United States had underestimated Hitler's power.

The British begged FDR for help. They needed destroyers to stop German submarines from attacking England and from cutting off the country's ocean supply routes.

Roosevelt knew the American public didn't want to get pulled into the war in Europe. Even if he decided to send aid, he would have to do it within the law. The Neutrality Acts, passed by Congress during the previous five years, were meant to keep the country out of the fighting.

The president called together Jackson and other advisers. Was there a way to support Great Britain?

The Destroyers for Bases Agreement
American Navy gunners show their British counterparts how to use guns aboard one of the World War I–era destroyers turned over to Great Britain in exchange for naval and air bases in North America. The photo was taken in September 1940 in a Canadian port.

Over several months, they developed a deal. Jackson gave FDR advice and worked out the legal framework so that the deal didn't violate U.S. law. The United States would provide Britain with fifty World War I navy destroyers to fight German submarines. In exchange, Britain would give the Americans the right to use military bases in the Caribbean Sea and western Atlantic Ocean. These bases would improve U.S. security, including its protection of the Panama Canal. The trade was called the Destroyers for Bases Agreement.

Jackson dreaded the United States' involvement in the war, but he was in favor of helping Britain. "I couldn't see how we could stand by and see England go down. If we could have those destroyers used to stop Hitler without their having to be manned by American boys, I was satisfied. ..."

After President Roosevelt announced the agreement, Congress and the public went along with few objections. Hitler's power had shocked and frightened them. If Britain fell, would Hitler attack the United States next?

Attorney General Duties
Attorney General Jackson (right) meets in May 1940 with Solicitor General Francis Biddle (1886–1968), who had succeeded Jackson in the position. Jackson had just announced plans to build up the national defense by fighting espionage and sabotage. Biddle was given responsibility for the Bureau of Immigration. In 1941, Biddle would succeed Jackson again, this time as attorney general.

Americans grew suspicious of foreigners who might cause trouble. They worried about sabotage of American weapon and airplane factories. The FBI received nearly three thousand complaints a day about suspected spies.

This kept Jackson and his Justice Department busy. Roosevelt directed Jackson to authorize wiretaps of phone calls so that the FBI could investigate espionage and sabotage. The president put the Justice Department in charge of controlling the borders and overseeing millions of aliens living in the country.

Jackson believed that the Department of Justice had to do everything possible to defend the country—without trampling citizens' rights. "In the process of upholding democratic ideals," he wrote, "we must not unwittingly destroy or impair what we are ... endeavoring to preserve."

His job wasn't easy. Besides advising Roosevelt as the possibility of war increased, Jackson often found himself in the middle of disagreements between Congress and executive branch departments. He had to attend social events with people he didn't like. It was all part of Washington politics. "The best thing about these Washington parties," he once said, "is that you see, for a few minutes, a lot of people with whom a few minutes is enough!"

Francis Biddle, who had taken over as solicitor general, noticed that Jackson wasn't happy. "He disliked the daily grind of administrative work, and

Throwing Boomerangs
Vice-presidential candidate Henry Wallace (right) shows Attorney General Jackson how to throw a boomerang in August 1940. Wallace (1888–1965) was FDR's secretary of agriculture (1933–1940) and became vice president when Roosevelt won his third term in November 1940. Wallace later broke from the Democrats and ran for president in 1948 on the Progressive Party ticket.

Lend-Lease
As part of the Lend-Lease program, the United States shipped twin-engine bombers and other military supplies to countries fighting Germany.

remembered the charmed days when he was arguing cases before the Court. ..."

Jackson tried to find time for his family, but it was hard to get away. He took short trips to see Mary at Smith College in Massachusetts and Bill at Yale University in Connecticut. He and Irene drove up to Jamestown to visit old friends and family, including Bob's mother, who was in failing health.

The fighting in Europe continued. The growing threat convinced Franklin Roosevelt to run for a third term instead of stepping down as he had planned. The voters reelected him in November 1940, the first and only time a U.S. president had been elected to three terms.

Robert Jackson missed FDR's inauguration in January 1941, sending Bill to stand in for him at inauguration events. Jackson had suffered what he first thought was a heart attack. Bob knew he might have inherited the Jackson heart. His father had died at age fifty-two from heart trouble. But the doctors told Bob it wasn't a heart attack, and they advised him to rest for a few weeks.

In his inaugural speech, President Roosevelt asked Congress to approve the Lend-Lease program, which would allow the shipment of more military supplies to the countries fighting Germany.

As attorney general, Jackson defended Lend-Lease against those who said it was illegal under international law. He argued that Germany had broken treaties by invading other countries and that the United States had the right to help these countries without entering the war itself.

Congress passed the Lend-Lease Act in March. The United States had taken a step closer to involvement in the war.

———◆———

In early June 1941, Roosevelt called Jackson into his office. The president had two Supreme Court positions to fill. Both Chief Justice Charles Evans Hughes and Associate Justice James McReynolds had retired.

When Justice McReynolds resigned in January, FDR had not filled his seat immediately. Jackson's name had come up then among the press and other Court watchers. At the time, Mary wrote her father from Smith College: "I hope you don't get appointed to the Supreme Court. ... I'd hate to see you retire leaving such important work [as attorney general] to one less competent and level-headed. I wish you could wait until someone else resigns when times are better and good men aren't so sorely needed."

Good News!
Jackson with Mary and Irene in their Washington apartment in June 1941, after President Roosevelt nominated him to the Supreme Court.

After Chief Justice Hughes's retirement announcement on June 2, the rumor mill and the press predicted that the president would finally name Jackson as chief justice. A *Washington Post* column said: "In New Deal circles it is taken for granted ... that the next Chief Justice of the United States will be Robert H. Jackson. ... No man in the President's entourage has more thoroughly earned promotion."

It was not to be. Roosevelt told Jackson the time wasn't right for him to be chief justice. At forty-nine, he was too young. Instead, the president was going to promote Associate Justice Harlan Stone to the chief justice position. Jackson would take Stone's seat as an associate justice, and Senator James Byrnes of South Carolina would take Justice McReynolds's seat.

Proud Dad
Jackson congratulates his son, Bill, upon his graduation from Yale University on June 17, 1941, soon after Jackson was nominated to the Supreme Court.

Jackson suspected that politics was behind Roosevelt's decision. The Republicans in Congress would be pleased with Republican Stone's promotion to chief justice. With war clouds thickening, the president needed their support.

Roosevelt added, "I think I will have another chance at appointment of a chief justice, at which time you'd already be over there and would be familiar with the job."

Jackson knew that Justice Stone had been ill and was close to retirement age, but he had heard Roosevelt's promises before.

Although he was disappointed, Jackson didn't show it. "Associate justice of the Supreme Court is a long ways from the farm in Spring Creek," he said to the president. "It's all that I'm entitled to."

The Senate approved Jackson's nomination to the Court by voice vote on July 7.

On July 11, 1941, after a cabinet meeting, President Roosevelt led Jackson into his study. The rest of the cabinet and many of Jackson's friends crowded into the room. Irene and Mary were at Bob's side. Bill missed the occasion

The Brand-New Justice
On July 11, 1941, President Roosevelt shakes Jackson's hand after he took the oath as associate justice of the Supreme Court in the White House. Irene and Mary, a student at Smith College, look on.

because he was traveling out West before starting Harvard Law School.

President Roosevelt joked that he wished he could cut his friend in half. Then Jackson could serve both in the cabinet and on the Supreme Court.

Jackson put his hand on the Bible once owned by his great-grandfather Elijah Jackson. The clerk of the Supreme Court administered the oath, and Robert Houghwout Jackson became the eighty-second associate justice of the Supreme Court.

CHAPTER SEVEN

The Eloquent Justice

On Monday, October 6, 1941—the first day of the Court's term—the justices gathered in the conference room of the Supreme Court building. Bob Jackson wore his new black judicial robe, a gift from the people who worked for him at the Justice Department.

By tradition, the nine justices shook hands and then lined up. Jackson heard the marshal's voice from the courtroom. "All rise," the marshal called out as he pounded his gavel.

On that cue, Jackson and the other justices entered the courtroom through three openings in the red velvet curtain. Jackson took his seat in the black upholstered chair at one end of the mahogany bench.

Jackson's first day on the bench lasted only four minutes. Chief Justice Harlan Stone cut short the session in memory of retired Justice Louis Brandeis, who had died the day before. Irene was among the spectators, along with six Jamestown friends.

Since Supreme Court justices have lifetime appointments, Bob Jackson figured he'd be living in Washington until he died or retired from the Court. He and Irene put their Jamestown house up for sale and bought a hundred-year-old house in McLean, Virginia, outside of Washington. The three-story white brick house, called Hickory Hill, came with six acres of land.

First Day
On October 6, 1941, the beginning of the Supreme Court's fall term, Jackson arrives in his convertible for his first day on the bench as an associate justice.

After several years in an apartment, Bob was glad to have more room. He brought down his chestnut mare, René, from Jamestown so that he could ride every day. Mary's horse came, too, so that she could ride when she was home from college.

Jackson hired a handyman to care for the horses and keep up the grounds, but he liked working in the stable and garden whenever he could. The swings hanging from the great, old trees were a perfect place to relax and think.

Family Portrait
The Jackson family and their dog Jerry outside their home in Jamestown in 1938. Soon after Jackson became a Supreme Court justice, he sold the Jamestown house and bought Hickory Hill in Virginia.

Although Bob Jackson's life was full of the things he enjoyed from his childhood and from Jamestown, he now lived in a completely different world. He was a friend of the president, and he and Irene attended dinners and parties with foreign ambassadors. He had a voice in decisions that affected millions of people. His photograph was regularly in national newspapers and magazines.

Jackson didn't let his fame go to his head. Soon after he became a Supreme Court justice, he wrote: "One must not judge men by their manners or their art any more than one may judge a horse by the harness he wears."

He went fishing with Hickory Hill's caretaker and the clerks from the Court's law library. On holidays, he invited the Court printers and janitors to his chambers for a drink. A secretary who worked for him said, "Justice Jackson treated everyone alike, whether you were an attorney, secretary, or diplomat."

Jackson settled into the routine of the Court. This was the kind of legal work he loved doing. To prepare for each oral argument, Jackson read the briefs in which the lawyers summarized their viewpoints. Then he studied law books about related court decisions.

When the time came to write an opinion, Jackson did it himself, unlike some justices whose law clerks did the work. Jackson asked his law clerk to check his draft and make suggestions. He considered it his responsibility as a justice to make up his own mind about each case. After nearly thirty years as a lawyer in Jamestown and in government, he was used to handling his own research and writing.

One of his law clerks later said that Jackson took time to polish his writing. "Although he seemed to write easily, he worked and reworked every opinion. He was not frustrated by the pursuit of perfection. ..."

Jackson stopped voting in elections when he took his seat on the Court. He thought judges should keep their personal views out of their official decisions. "Something does happen to a man when he puts on a judicial robe, and I think it ought to." A judge's job was to decide "other people's controversies, instead of waging them."

Hickory Hill
The Jackson home in McLean, Virginia. During the Civil War, the house served as General George McClellan's Union Army headquarters. After Robert Jackson's death, his family sold the house to then-Senator John F. Kennedy, the future president (1961–1963). He later sold it to his brother Robert F. Kennedy, who was attorney general from 1961 to 1964 and a U.S. senator from 1965 until his assassination in 1968. Robert Kennedy's family owned the house for more than fifty years.

Working on the Shrubbery
Although he hired a handyman to care for the grounds at Hickory Hill, Jackson enjoyed working outside.

Sunday, December 7, 1941, was a brisk and windy day in Washington. Bob Jackson was relaxing at Hickory Hill. He had some reading to do, and he had turned on his radio for background music.

The music stopped abruptly. An announcer's voice interrupted. Japanese planes had bombed Pearl Harbor in Hawaii. Planes and ships in America's Pacific Fleet were destroyed. Later Jackson learned that more than three thousand Americans had been killed or wounded.

Jackson was shaken. He knew war was possible. Yet no one had been ready for Japan's attack that December day. The United States had underestimated Hitler's

Germany, and it had misjudged Japan's power, too.

Within days, Congress declared war on Japan, Germany, and Italy. Jackson had never thought that war solved anything, but this time was different. The United States had to fight. "The first [world] war seemed to me preventable—the second did not ...," he said. "The former was evil enough; the latter could not be tolerated in a civilized world."

Jackson felt frustrated sitting on the Supreme Court while the country faced a terrible crisis. The day after the Pearl Harbor attack, he listened to oral arguments about whether country-club members should be taxed on their golf fees. "I sputtered much about hearing such a damn petty question all day with the world in flames," Jackson said later.

The Bombing of Pearl Harbor
Sunday morning, December 7, 1941, Pearl Harbor, Hawaii. Naval ships USS West Virginia and USS Tennessee burn after Japanese planes bombed them. In the two-hour surprise attack on the U.S. Naval Base, more than two thousand Americans were killed and over one thousand were wounded. Since the early 1930s, Japan had become increasingly aggressive and had already invaded several Asian neighbors, including China.

He suggested to President Roosevelt that he was willing to resign from the Court and return to the executive branch to help with the war effort. The president told him to stay where he was because his work on the Court had long-lasting importance. Once again, FDR hinted that he would make Jackson chief justice in the future.

War!
On December 8, 1941, President Roosevelt signs the war declaration against Japan passed by Congress. In his address to a joint session of Congress that day, he called December 7 "a date which will live in infamy."

Like everyone else, Bob and Irene Jackson adjusted their lives to wartime. They joined millions of Americans in planting a Victory Garden. By growing their own vegetables, they freed up farm-grown vegetables to supply the troops overseas.

Irene trained to be a volunteer air spotter near Hickory Hill. She identified planes flying overhead by their appearance and engine sound, keeping watch for enemy aircraft. Then she reported the information to the army, which guarded against air invasion.

With gas in short supply, Jackson often worked at home instead of making the twenty-minute drive into the Supreme Court every day. He used his horse to run errands close to his house in Virginia.

In May of 1942, Bob's mother died of cancer. After their visit to Jamestown for her funeral, the Jacksons took fewer trips to New York. Gas rationing made it difficult to drive long distances. Instead of going to Jamestown for part of their summer vacation, Bob and Irene stayed in Washington.

Reunion
After his mother's death in 1942, Jackson visited his sisters and their families in Jamestown. Left to right: Jackson; sister Ella Springer; sister Helen Adams holding Karen Ingeman, Ella's granddaughter; Ruth Springer Ingeman, Ella's daughter; Harold Adams, Helen's son; Erie Springer, Ella's husband; and Kenneth Ingeman, Ella's son-in-law.

After America entered the war, federal, state, and local governments passed new laws and regulations. Critics challenged these wartime laws, charging that the laws took away citizens' rights. The Supreme Court was asked to decide how much power the government should have in time of war.

One case involved two girls who lived near Charleston, West Virginia. Each morning at their tiny Slip Hill Grade School, two dozen children recited the Pledge of Allegiance to a picture of an American flag. Their class did not have a real flag until after the war began.

Gathie Barnett, age eleven, and her nine-year-old sister, Marie, stood quietly with arms at their sides while their schoolmates said the Pledge. The two girls belonged to a religious group called the Jehovah's Witnesses. The Witnesses believed it was wrong to worship anything other than God. That included the American flag.

One day in the spring of 1942, their principal sent Gathie and Marie home for refusing to salute the flag. He was enforcing a new rule by the West Virginia Board of Education that required all children to honor the country by saluting the flag and reciting the Pledge. Anyone who refused was not allowed to attend school.

A lawyer at the Jehovah's Witnesses headquarters in New York heard about the Barnett girls. This was the case he had been looking for—a chance to challenge laws that prevented the Witnesses from practicing their religion. He sued the

The Barnett Sisters
Marie and Gathie Barnett, two young Jehovah's Witnesses from West Virginia who refused to salute the U.S. flag at their school.

Board of Education on the Barnetts' behalf.

The court in West Virginia agreed with the Barnetts. It said that the Constitution's First Amendment guaranteed freedom of religion. Children could not be expelled from school for refusing to salute the flag or say the Pledge. The judges ordered the school to let Gathie and Marie come back.

West Virginia's Board of Education appealed the case to the Supreme Court. On March 11, 1943, Robert Jackson and the other justices heard oral arguments for *West Virginia State Board of Education v. Barnette*. The Supreme Court misspelled the family's name.

The case caught the public's attention. The nation was at war, and most Americans felt patriotic. The Jehovah's Witnesses were unpopular because they opposed the war and refused to serve in the military. A *New York Times* column called the Jehovah's Witnesses "militant and thoroughly unpatriotic, even subversive."

Growing up in Frewsburg, Robert Jackson had learned to respect people with different beliefs, both religious and political. He didn't think the state of West Virginia should be allowed to force people to say what they didn't believe.

The Supreme Court announced its decision on Flag Day, June 14, 1943. Six justices, including Jackson, ruled that states could not require schoolchildren to recite the Pledge or salute the flag. The three dissenting justices said that it was more important to have national unity during time of war. They wrote that the state had the right to promote good citizenship with flag-salute rules.

Robert Jackson wrote the Court's majority opinion. He stated that allowing the compulsory flag salute was like saying the "Bill of Rights which guards the individual's right to speak his own mind, left it open to public authorities to compel him to utter what is not in his mind."

It made no difference if the country was at war and the flag was a patriotic symbol. The Barnett girls weren't doing any harm to others when they refused to salute.

"If there is any fixed star in our constitutional constellation," he wrote, "it is that no official, high or petty, can prescribe what shall be orthodox in politics, nationalism, religion, or other matters of opinion or force citizens to confess by word or act their faith therein."

Jackson's opinion received widespread praise. The *New York Times* called it "one of the most notable writings in the court's history."

Despite his opinion in the Barnetts' favor, Robert Jackson didn't believe that the First Amendment gave a person or group unlimited rights. "I think the limits begin to operate whenever activities begin to affect or collide with liberties of others or of the public."

He ruled against the Jehovah's Witnesses in other cases. In one, Jackson supported an Ohio town's ban on doorbell ringing. Many people in Struthers worked a night shift and slept during the day. In Jackson's view, a citizen had the right to protect his sleep from a Witness ringing his doorbell to hand out religious materials. The Supreme Court majority disagreed with Jackson, ruling that the town's law interfered with the Jehovah's Witnesses' freedom of religion and press.

In Jackson's mind, the Supreme Court was responsible for balancing the rights of individual citizens and the voice of the majority. "The question simmers down to one of the extent to which majority rule will be set aside ...," he wrote. "The power of the Court to protect individual or minority rights has on the other side of the coin the power to restrain the majority."

Finding that balance wasn't always easy, especially when the country's security was at risk. In 1944, the Supreme Court took on such a case.

Fred Korematsu was born in 1919 in Oakland, California. His parents were immigrants from Japan. The young man worked as a welder in the San Francisco shipyards. After the Pearl Harbor attack in December 1941, his life was turned upside down.

Americans were worried that Japan might invade the United States. They feared that Japanese spies could easily blend in with the many West Coast residents of Japanese descent. These spies might signal the Japanese fleet to attack the coastline, or they could sabotage the region's aircraft factories, which were important to fighting the war.

In February 1942, President Franklin Roosevelt issued an executive order allowing the War Department to set up military zones throughout the western United States, including California. The military began to evacuate everyone of Japanese ancestry from these zones. The people were sent to internment camps away from the West Coast. According to the order, the government could hold people at these centers until officials decided it was safe to release them.

Fred Korematsu was ordered to leave his home in San Leandro, California. More than 110,000 others received the same order. Like Fred, the majority of them were American citizens.

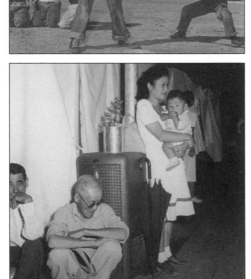

Japanese Internment

The Manzanar Relocation Center, 250 miles from Los Angeles, California, was one of ten camps set up in the United States during World War II to intern people of Japanese descent. More than ten thousand people were held at this camp, operated from 1942 to 1945. Two-thirds of them were American citizens.

In this 1943 photograph by Francis Stewart, "Sixth-Grade Boys Play Softball" (top), children entertain themselves at Manzanar. Barracks are visible in the background.

In Dorothea Lange's photograph from 1942 "Inside a Barrack," a family makes a temporary home, separated from other families by only cloth partitions.

Korematsu had an Italian American girlfriend, and he didn't want to leave her. Why should he have to report to a camp? He was an American citizen and he had done nothing to hurt his country.

Fred tried to avoid the police. He even had plastic surgery on his face so that he looked less Japanese. But in May 1942, the police picked him up. A federal district court found Korematsu guilty of violating the military order and sent him to an internment camp in Utah.

After his conviction, Korematsu filed an appeal challenging his exclusion from his hometown. His lawyer argued in court that the Constitution protected an American citizen from being locked up without any evidence that he committed a crime. Korematsu lost his first appeal, and he then took his case to the Supreme Court.

On October 11, 1944, the Supreme Court justices heard oral arguments for *Korematsu v. U.S.* Two months later, they announced their decision.

The justices voted 6–3 against Fred Korematsu. Justice Hugo Black wrote the majority opinion. He said that in time of war, the government had the power to move people of Japanese ancestry away from the West Coast. This protected the nation from threats of sabotage and spying.

Robert Jackson disagreed. In his dissenting opinion, he stated that Fred Korematsu should be freed. Jackson said that the Constitution didn't give the president, Congress, or the military the power to move people or arrest them because of their race.

He wrote: "Korematsu ... has been convicted of an act not commonly a crime. It consists merely of being present in the state whereof he is a citizen, near the place where he was born, and where all his life he has lived. ... Here is an attempt to make an otherwise innocent act a crime merely because this prisoner is the son of parents as to whom he had no choice, and belongs to a race from which there is no way to resign."

Jackson was afraid that the Court's majority opinion set a dangerous precedent. If the Supreme Court allowed this evacuation based only on race just because the military said it was necessary, "then we may as well say that any military order will be constitutional and have done with it."

He went on, "I do not think they [the courts] may be asked to execute a military expedient that has no place in law under the Constitution. I would reverse the judgment and discharge the prisoner."

Robert Jackson's opinions impressed people who followed the Supreme Court. His writing didn't have the complex legal language that some justices used.

His fellow justice Felix Frankfurter, a former Harvard law professor, said of Jackson: "He wrote as he talked, and he talked as he felt. ... His speech breaks through the printed page. He was one of those rare men whose spoken word survives in type."

Throughout the war years, Jackson noticed increasing tension among the justices. Franklin Roosevelt had named seven of the nine justices to the Court, and he expected his appointees to have similar opinions. Instead, the justices often sharply disagreed, with some votes being close 5–4 splits.

During oral arguments one day, a lawyer was worried about the time he had left to speak. He asked the justices, "May I be advised how much time remains? The clock at the front and the one at the rear of the courtroom seem not to agree." Jackson wryly replied, "That's the influence of this Court."

The justices often had opposing ideas about the Supreme Court's role in government. Jackson generally believed in judicial restraint. In most situations, he thought that the Supreme Court should support laws passed by Congress and the state legislatures. The people had elected the lawmakers as their representatives, and the Court should respect that. The exception was when the law unreasonably infringed on a person's rights. In Jackson's view, this had been the situation in the *Barnette* and *Korematsu* cases.

Other justices such as Hugo Black and William Douglas were more willing to strike down laws. They were in favor of using the Court's power to make changes in existing government policies.

Jackson disliked the bickering and power struggles among the justices. "I didn't realize the situation on the court to be just what it was," he said later, "or perhaps I would have remained as Attorney General for a time and then returned to private practice."

By early 1945, Jackson saw that World War II would soon end. The Allies' military victories in Europe and the Pacific had weakened the Axis powers of Germany, Italy, and Japan. People felt optimistic about victory.

On Thursday afternoon, April 12, 1945, Jackson was in his stable at Hickory Hill with his horse, René. His handyman came back from town. Had Jackson heard? President Roosevelt had suffered a stroke. He was dead.

The news stunned Jackson. He and Irene had seen Roosevelt at a dinner a few weeks earlier. The president had seemed worn out then, but this was unexpected.

Later in the evening of April 12, Jackson joined two dozen officials in the cabinet room at the White House. He stood with cabinet members, congressmen, and other Supreme Court justices as Vice President Harry Truman took the presidential oath.

The next afternoon Jackson spoke at a memorial service for FDR held at the Justice Department. "No other event could bow so many human heads in a common sorrow and a sense of personal loss," he said. By the end of his speech, his emotions caught up with him and he could barely get out the words. "We are glad that he lived the high moments when he could see that his efforts have led our country to the very threshold of victory both in Europe and in the Orient."

Franklin Delano Roosevelt's Funeral
FDR's flag-draped casket passes a military honor guard on April 15, 1945, in Hyde Park, New York.

On Saturday, Bob and Irene went to the White House for a short funeral service in the East Room. Then they boarded the funeral train to the Roosevelt family home in Hyde Park, New York. The train carried the president's family, President Harry Truman, the cabinet, Supreme Court justices, members of Congress, and other officials from Roosevelt's administration.

When the train arrived in Hyde Park the next morning, the day was clear and chilly. The lilacs and apple trees on the Roosevelt estate were in bloom, and birds sang in the tall oak trees. FDR was buried in a garden close to the house where he had been born.

Franklin Roosevelt had brought Robert H. Jackson to Washington and set him on his government journey. Now he was gone.

CHAPTER EIGHT

The Case Against the Nazis

Late on an April afternoon soon after Roosevelt's funeral, Robert Jackson received a phone call from the White House. It was Samuel Rosenman, a long-time adviser to FDR. Now he was advising President Harry Truman.

Rosenman needed to see Jackson, but it was best if no one spotted the justice at the White House. Rosenman would come over to the Supreme Court.

Jackson welcomed Rosenman into his chambers, and Rosenman got right to the point. Before Roosevelt's death, the president had begun talks with the Allies about the punishment of Adolf Hitler and other Nazi Party leaders. They discussed a military trial after the war ended, involving the United States, Great Britain, France, and the Soviet Union. That time was near. Allied troops had entered Germany from all sides. So far, no agreement for trials had been worked out.

The Allied Leaders Meet
Left to right: Prime Minister Winston Churchill of Great Britain, President Franklin D. Roosevelt, and Marshal Joseph Stalin of the Soviet Union at the Yalta Conference in February 1945. At this meeting held on the Crimean Peninsula in the Black Sea, the Allied leaders discussed how to deal with Germany after the war. Roosevelt died two months later.

Rosenman went on to say that President Truman admired Jackson as an experienced trial lawyer. Would the justice prosecute the American case against these Nazi leaders?

Bob Jackson realized that this trial broke new legal ground. For the first time, a country's leaders would be tried for aggressively starting and waging a war. As the chief prosecutor, he would represent the United States government in a historic international trial. Jackson couldn't resist the challenge.

He considered how he could juggle the trial's duties with his work on the Supreme

Court. The current Court term would be over soon. Jackson expected the war trial to be finished by fall. He could be back at the Supreme Court by the time the next term started in October.

Harry S. Truman
(1884–1972)
Vice President Truman became president when FDR died in April 1945. He ran for reelection in 1948 against Thomas Dewey, the Republican candidate, and won. Truman remained in office until 1953.

Still, he knew that Chief Justice Stone wouldn't approve of his taking on a responsibility separate from Supreme Court duties. Jackson wondered whether he should resign from the Court. He discussed it with President Truman, who said he didn't want Jackson to resign. After their conversation, Jackson agreed to become chief U.S. counsel for the military trial.

Within days, Adolf Hitler killed himself in a Berlin bunker as the Soviets moved into the city. A few key Nazi leaders also committed suicide when they realized they were defeated. Germany surrendered, and the war in Europe ended.

The Survivors
Starving prisoners at the Nazi concentration camp in Ebensee, Austria. A U.S. Army photographer took this photograph after American troops liberated the camp in May 1945. Prisoners had been dying of starvation and illness at the rate of two thousand per week.

The Allied armies took control of different sections of Germany. The American, British, and Soviet armies captured several high-ranking Nazis in their sections. Some German leaders surrendered to the Americans and British because they feared being captured and mistreated by the Soviets.

Most people in the United States and Europe saw no reason to bother with a trial of the Nazi prisoners. They wanted the men killed or imprisoned. Even Winston Churchill and Joseph Stalin, the British and Soviet leaders, initially called for immediate executions.

The demands for revenge grew louder after the Allies entered Nazi concentration camps. People were horrified by photographs of emaciated prisoners and dead bodies piled in heaps and by the reports of torture rooms and gas chambers.

The London Conference
Four representatives from each of the four Allied nations sit around a square table in London to prepare for the war trial, July 1945. The American team sits along the right-hand side of the table. Jackson, in a bow tie, is third from right.

Jackson understood their anger and disgust. The Nazis deserved punishment, but Jackson wanted the punishment carried out fairly. He wrote in a report to President Truman that it was important to "punish only the right men and for the right reasons."

In Jackson's opinion, a trial was the best way, as long as it wasn't rigged to find the defendants guilty. No one should be convicted unless the evidence proved it. That meant that an accused person might be found innocent.

With the public demanding quick action, Jackson wasted no time. When the Supreme Court term ended in mid-June, he flew to London to work out trial details with the Allies. In addition to his staff of lawyers and assistants, he took along his son, Bill, as his personal assistant. Bill had recently completed Harvard Law School and joined the U.S. Navy as an ensign.

At the London Conference, the Americans, British, French, and Soviets met around a large square table. Each country's representatives, most of whom were lawyers, sat along one of the four sides. They decided on the crimes for which the Nazis would be tried. Then they discussed how to conduct the trial.

The Allies agreed that the defendants should not be allowed to use the courtroom to spread Nazi propaganda or to rally their supporters in Germany. But the representatives had trouble deciding on the guidelines of the trial. The four countries had different rules about the rights of an accused person, the roles of judges and lawyers, and the presentation of evidence.

Jackson took the lead in finding agreement. He pressed the Allies to use an approach like the American and British legal systems. For more than a month, he struggled to bring everyone together.

The Soviets were particularly stubborn and difficult. The Russian people had suffered greatly when Germany invaded their country, and they wanted harsh retribution.

Finally, the four Allies produced a plan. Jackson wished the negotiations hadn't taken so long, although he was pleased with the result, a two-part document. The first part, called the Agreement, set up the International Military Tribunal to try and punish the leading European war criminals. The second part, called the Charter, described their crimes:

Rounding Up Jews
A German photograph shows Jews being removed from their community at gunpoint. This photograph, taken by the Nazis and found by Allied investigators after the war, was used as evidence against the Nazi leaders in the Nuremberg Trial.

Crimes Against Peace, for planning, starting, and waging an illegal war. The Allies charged that the Nazis broke treaties with other European countries and then invaded them. The war was aggressive. It was not waged in self-defense.

War Crimes, for mistreating prisoners of war and civilians in the invaded countries. This included murdering people or using them as slave labor and destroying and stealing their property.

Crimes Against Humanity, for murder, enslavement, and other inhumane treatment of civilians. This included persecuting people based on their politics, race, or religion. The Allies accused the Nazis of killing anyone who opposed them before and during the war. The Nazis rounded up and killed millions of Jews, Gypsies, and other minority groups.

According to the Charter, each of the four countries would send one judge and one alternate to sit on the Tribunal. The judges would decide to acquit or convict the defendants based on the evidence presented by prosecutors from each nation. The accused were allowed to choose their own lawyers to present their defense.

On August 8, 1945, the four Allies signed the London Agreement and Charter. Robert Jackson signed for the United States.

Francis Biddle, who was appointed by President Truman as an American judge on the Tribunal, later wrote: "Robert Jackson's tireless energy and skill had finally brought the four nations together—a really extraordinary feat. ..."

But some legal experts and politicians criticized the London Agreement. They believed that the Nazi leaders should not be tried for waging an aggressive war. In their view, aggressive warfare wasn't considered a crime at the time the Nazis committed it. According to American legal standards, defendants can't be tried for acts committed *before* those acts become crimes.

Six days after the signing, Japan surrendered when the United States dropped atomic bombs on the cities of Hiroshima and Nagasaki. With the end of fighting in the Pacific, World War II was over. It had lasted six years and involved more than seventy countries.

———◆———

Nuremberg, Germany, after the war ended. Ninety percent of the city was destroyed by Allied bombings from 1943 to 1945.

The trial was scheduled to begin in the fall, and it would be a huge undertaking. Hundreds of people would be involved. The four Allies' prosecution staffs had lawyers, investigators, translators, and clerks. In addition, there were the judges and their aides, soldiers, interpreters, and court workers.

At the London Conference, Jackson had volunteered to find a place to hold the trial. The U.S. Army suggested Nuremberg, a city in southern Germany in the area controlled by the Americans. American and British bombing leveled most German cities during the final months of the war. Nuremberg was badly damaged, but it had a standing courthouse and a prison.

When he first saw Nuremberg, Bob Jackson was shocked at the destruction. Piles of stone rubble remained where buildings once stood. The city had no public transportation or phones. The water system was broken, and electricity wasn't reliable.

As a military car drove him through the city, Jackson smelled decomposing bodies. Someone told him there were at least twenty thousand bodies under the rubble. The survivors wandered the city without enough food and clothing, and many lived in the ruins of bombed-out buildings.

Jackson thought about the huge Nazi rallies that Hitler once held in Nuremberg. Now Germany's dictator was dead, and the remaining Nazi leaders would face justice here.

The imposing Palace of Justice seemed to be the best place for the trial. The light-colored sandstone building occupied three city blocks and contained a courtroom, space for offices, and a jail for the prisoners.

Part of the roof was missing and windows were broken. The Army promised to make repairs in time for the trial. During the next few weeks, German prisoners did most of the construction, renovating the courtroom and offices. Carpenters built a wooden tunnel connecting the jail and the courtroom so that guards could securely move the Nazi defendants each day.

The Palace of Justice
in Nuremberg as it looked during the proceedings of the International Military Tribunal from 1945 to 1946. The building complex contained offices and a courthouse. The jail was located in the wings of the building behind the section visible from the street. Trials are still held today in Courtroom 600, where the Nuremberg trials were conducted, and the courtroom is open to tourists on weekends.

The U.S. Army was in charge of housing, too. Jackson stayed a few miles out of the city where there had been less bombing damage. He, son Bill, and his secretary, Elsie Douglas, settled into a large house with three stories and an attic. The house had rooms for meetings, a dining table that seated twenty, and several fancy bathrooms. Outside, Jackson was delighted to find gardens on the two acres of grounds as well as tennis and volleyball courts.

The Army didn't allow family members to visit or live in Nuremberg. Besides concerns about security, the military didn't want to deal with extra mouths to feed since food was in short supply in Germany. Jackson adopted this policy for his prosecution staff, too. Bill had been married for a year to Nancy Roosevelt,

Courtroom
Before: September 1945. Workers repair the area near the judges' bench.
***After:** November 14, 1945. With the courtroom renovated, Robert Jackson addresses the judges from the lawyers' podium (right) during pretrial proceedings.*

President Theodore Roosevelt's granddaughter, but neither she nor Irene would join their husbands in Nuremberg.

Jackson was assigned a bodyguard, Sergeant Moritz Fuchs, a twenty-year-old soldier who moved into the house. Jackson wasn't used to having someone follow him around like a shadow. "I can't go out or stay in except under guard," he wrote Irene. "A jeep load of soldiers follows my car night and morning in addition to Moritz. ... Every place you go requires a pass."

The Army worried about Germans who might disrupt the trial, harm those involved, or free the Nazi defendants. A high wall and hedge with barbed wire surrounded Jackson's house, and four soldiers stood guard at a gatehouse. A military driver drove him around, sometimes in a Mercedes that had belonged to one of the defendants, the Nazi foreign minister Joachim von Ribbentrop.

Jackson's next problem was running a trial in which four different languages were spoken: English, German, Russian, and French. Translation was sure to slow down the proceedings. Usually whenever a person spoke a line, an interpreter had to translate it into each of the other three languages. Everyone waited until the interpreter got to his or her language.

Fortunately, Jackson heard about a new system that made translations more quickly. The company that developed it, IBM, agreed to set up the system for free in the Nuremberg courtroom.

Each person in the courtroom wore headphones, which he or she could switch to one of the four languages. Translators sat behind a glass barrier in the courtroom. As a speaker addressed the court through a microphone, the interpreters immediately translated the words into the other three languages. Everyone heard the translation through his or her headphones at the same time.

Translating System
A German woman demonstrates the new translating equipment used by trial participants and observers in the Nuremberg courtroom. Interpreters sat behind a glass barrier in the courtroom and translated testimony. Listeners heard the translation through their earphones. This system for translating several languages simultaneously was new in 1945. Today it is used in the United Nations.

Before the trial started, Jackson and his team had to collect and organize the evidence to prove their case against the Nazi leaders. "We must establish incredible events by credible evidence," Jackson wrote in a report to President Truman.

The Army and other U.S. intelligence services collected tens of thousands of Nazi documents. They found them in government buildings, military headquarters, and houses. The Nazis had hidden papers behind false walls, stashed them in salt mines, and buried them in the ground. Investigators also discovered millions of feet of motion-picture film and thousands of photographs taken by the Nazis. They interviewed scores of witnesses. Useful information came from underground groups that had operated in France, Poland, Holland, Denmark, and Belgium during the war.

The Germans kept meticulous records. Their own words were the strongest evidence against them. Jackson was amazed. "I did not think men would ever be so foolish as to put in writing some of the things the Germans did put in writing."

As prosecutors from the four Allied countries studied the evidence, they compiled their list of defendants. Hermann Goering was second-in-command under Hitler and head of the air force. Rudolf Hess had been Hitler's deputy before parachuting into Britain in 1941 to negotiate peace, apparently without Hitler's consent. The British immediately imprisoned him. Albert Speer was minister of war production. Ernst Kaltenbrunner was head of the security

The Nazi Leadership
Adolf Hitler and his closest aides at a Nazi Party event in Nuremberg, Germany, in the 1930s. Left to right: Hitler; Hermann Goering (1893–1946), head of the air force; Joseph Goebbels (1897–1945), propaganda minister; Rudolf Hess (1894–1987), Hitler's deputy. Hitler and Goebbels committed suicide in the spring of 1945 as the Russian army closed in on Berlin. Goering surrendered after their deaths. Hess had been captured by the British in 1941.

police and concentration-camp system. Nearly two dozen other names joined the list.

By now, Jackson realized that his timetable had been wrong. The trial was unlikely to start until November. He wanted to see it through to the end, but that meant he would miss the beginning of the next Court term.

Jackson knew this wouldn't please some of the other justices already grumbling about his absence. Their workload would be heavier without him there. If any cases were 4–4 ties, they would have to be carried over until he returned. A few justices had criticized him for accepting the Nuremberg position.

Fellow justice William Douglas later wrote, "It was a gross violation of separation of powers to put a Justice in charge of an executive function. I thought, and I think [Justices] Stone and Black agreed, that if Bob did that, he should resign."

Jackson talked to President Truman and again offered to resign from the Supreme Court. Truman told him to stay on the Court and to continue with the trial in Nuremberg.

Jackson had to face that he'd be away from friends and family longer than he had planned. In early October he wrote Irene on her birthday. "I hope you had a good trip to Jamestown. Tell me about it. The people there I know and am interested to hear about. The people here are strangers to you and mostly to me."

When Robert Jackson agreed to be the chief American counsel, he hadn't expected how hard the task would be. "This is the first case I have ever tried," he said, "when I had first to persuade others that a court should be established, help negotiate its establishment, and when that was done, not only prepare my case but find myself a courtroom in which to try it."

The Nuremberg Trial was about to begin.

View of the Nuremberg Trial Courtroom
The eight judges sit on the left with the court staff below them. Across the courtroom on the right in the photograph, the defendants in the dock face the judges. The defendants' lawyers sit at tables in front of the dock. The prosecutors' tables are directly behind the lawyers' podium in the center of the photograph. At the rear of the courtroom, visitors sit in the balcony and reporters sit below.

CHAPTER NINE

The Nuremberg Trial

On Wednesday, November 21, 1945, Robert Jackson took his chair at the American prosecutors' table in the Nuremberg courtroom. It was the second day of the trial. The day before, prosecutors from each of the four Allied countries read the charges against the defendants.

Today Jackson would make his opening address before the International Military Tribunal. He spent weeks writing the speech, much of it by candlelight. The house at Lindenstrasse 33 didn't have enough electric light in the evenings when he had time to write.

Jackson depended on Bill and other prosecution lawyers to collect the documents he needed to prepare his speech. He organized the notes in piles on a bed in the spare room. One day, the housekeeper left open the windows in the room, and a storm blew hundreds of papers out the window and soaked the rest with rain. Jackson had to start again.

He crafted his speech to show how the Nazis plotted to take over Europe. Jackson didn't intend to blame all Germans, just the leaders. He would be addressing the eight judges, but he meant his words for the press and public, too.

Six hundred reporters from around the world were covering the trial. Jackson expected newspapers to quote the speech and cameramen to film it for movie theater newsreels. He hoped that press reports revealed to the public exactly what the Nazis had done and how they had done it.

On the trial's second day, the dark-paneled courtroom was packed. Behind Jackson, the room had seats for four hundred reporters and visitors. Nearly two hundred more people filled the front section of the courtroom—the judges, prosecutors, guards, interpreters, court recorders, and defendants. The defendants had been allowed to choose their own German lawyers. These men sat in front of the dock wearing traditional lawyer robes.

Jackson watched as an elevator behind the dock brought the defendants up from the jail to the second-floor courtroom. A line of American military policemen in white helmets kept guard along the back and side of the dock. Twenty men settled into their seats.

Hermann Goering sat in the first row of the dock. As Hitler's second-in-command, he was the most senior Nazi leader alive and in custody. He strode confidently into the courtroom, wearing riding boots and his double-breasted uniform. Army guards had removed the uniform's military insignias.

Two defendants were missing from the dock that day. Ernst Kaltenbrunner, the head of the security police, was recovering from a stroke in an army hospital. Martin Bormann, a top Nazi Party official, had never been caught. Although many assumed he was dead, he was to be tried in absentia.

Everyone rose as the eight Tribunal judges filed into the courtroom and took their chairs behind the raised bench, each sitting in front of his nation's flag. As civilians, six wore black judicial robes. The two Soviets wore their army uniforms.

All but two of the men were experienced judges. One French judge was a law professor. Francis Biddle, the American judge, served for less than a year as a federal judge and had been a former U.S. solicitor general and attorney general. The American alternate, John J. Parker, was a federal judge.

The presiding judge was sixty-five-year-old Lord Geoffrey Lawrence of Great Britain. Seated at the middle of the bench, Lord Lawrence looked across the courtroom toward the dock. As he read a name, each of the twenty defendants moved to the microphone in the center of the dock. The judge asked the man whether he pleaded guilty or not guilty.

Hermann Goering tried to make a speech. "Before I answer the question of the Tribunal whether or not I am guilty ..."

Lord Lawrence cut him off. "I informed the Court that defendants were not entitled to make a statement. You must plead guilty or not guilty."

Goering stared at the judges. "I declare myself in the sense of the Indictment not guilty."

The rest of the defendants pleaded *nicht schuldig*, not guilty.

Prisoners in the Dock
The twenty-one defendants sit in two rows, guarded by American military police in white helmets. Two defendants are out of view at the far end of the front row. The twenty-second defendant was Martin Bormann, missing and tried in absentia.

Judges on the Bench
Four of the eight judges, left to right: General I. T. Nikitchenko (Russian judge), Norman Birkett (British judge), Lord Geoffrey Lawrence (British judge and the Tribunal's presiding judge), and Francis Biddle (American judge).

Jackson at the Podium
Robert Jackson addresses the Tribunal. His secretary, Elsie Douglas, sits to his right. Behind his right arm is American prosecution lawyer Thomas Dodd. Dodd (1907–1971) was elected to the U.S. Senate from Connecticut in 1958.

Then Lord Lawrence said, "I will now call upon the Chief Prosecutor for the United States of America."

Robert Jackson stepped to the lectern. Facing the judges, he began his opening address. He occasionally glanced at the pages of his speech as he spoke. But he had gone over it so many times that he almost knew the speech by heart.

"That four great nations, flushed with victory and stung with injury stay the hand of vengeance and voluntarily submit their captive enemies to the judgment of the law is one of the most significant tributes that Power has ever paid to reason."

Jackson made clear that the trial must be fair. "We must never forget that the record on which we judge these defendants today is the record on which history will judge us tomorrow. To pass these defendants a poisoned chalice is to put it to our own lips as well."

Whenever the red light on the lectern came on, Jackson paused. This was the interpreters' signal that he was speaking too fast, and they had fallen behind in the translation.

As he continued, Jackson described how the Nazi Party under Adolf Hitler had plotted to take control of Germany. Once the Nazis accomplished that, they planned a war to conquer Europe and the United States. "This war did not just happen," said Jackson. "It was planned and prepared for over a long period of time and with no small skill and cunning."

After the lunch break, Jackson went on with his speech. He detailed the Nazis' crimes against the Jews. "Of the 9,600,000 Jews who lived in Nazi-dominated Europe, 60 percent are authoritatively estimated to have perished. ... History does not record a crime ever perpetrated against so many victims or one ever carried out with such calculated cruelty."

He turned toward the dock. The defendants listened intently through their headphones. It was the first time they'd seen how much evidence the Allies had against them. Some glared at Jackson. Hermann Goering busily scribbled notes.

"We have here the surviving top politicians, militarists, financiers, diplomats, administrators, and propagandists, of the Nazi movement," said Jackson. "Who was responsible for these crimes if they were not?"

As he came to the conclusion, Jackson laid out his hope for the future. "The ultimate step in avoiding periodic wars, which are inevitable in a system of international lawlessness, is to make statesmen responsible to law."

The speech lasted four hours. Jackson was exhausted, but he felt it had gone well.

The audience in the courtroom thought so, too. Many people praised the eloquence and power of his words. The *Washington Post* called the speech a "brilliant opening statement."

CBS radio broadcaster William Shirer wrote, "It is more than one of the great speeches of our time. It is by far the most adequate summing up of the Nazi-German monstrosity yet committed to our language."

Jackson's prosecution team included twenty-three other lawyers. Working with the rest of his staff, they had spent the months before the trial gathering and organizing evidence. The Americans planned to prove their case by presenting the Nazis' own documents. The prosecutors had reviewed one hundred thousand captured documents. By the trial's end, they would use four thousand of them and eighteen hundred photographs as evidence against the Nazis.

Some members of the prosecution team had initially argued for making the case with eyewitness testimony. Jackson agreed that live witnesses would grab the attention of the spectators, including the press. But he didn't want to weaken the case with witnesses whose hate for the defendants made them less believable.

When a few Nazis in the dock offered to testify against their fellow defendants, Jackson refused. People might think the trial was unfair if the prosecution

Photographic Evidence
This German photograph was used in the trial as evidence against the Nazi leaders. It shows Jewish men, women, and children about to be executed.

seemed to be making secret deals. The American case would be based on documents, not eyewitnesses.

For the first several days of the trial, the American prosecutors read document evidence aloud in court. Jackson saw that this slowed down the trial. The prosecution team decided it was time to rouse the courtroom with more dramatic evidence.

On the afternoon of November 29, Thomas Dodd stepped to the lectern. A former FBI agent and Justice Department lawyer, thirty-eight-year-old Dodd introduced a one-hour movie, *Nazi Concentration Camps*. It was compiled from film the Allied military photographers had taken when the American and British armies freed the concentration camps.

Concentration-Camp Ovens

Incinerators at Buchenwald concentration camp in Germany used to dispose of dead prisoners' bodies. American troops found charred remains in these ovens when they liberated the camp in April 1945. This photograph was taken by a U.S. Army photographer.

"We intend to prove that each and every one of these defendants knew of the existence of these concentration camps;" Dodd announced, "that fear and terror and nameless horror of the concentration camps were instruments by which the defendants retained power and suppressed opposition of their policies, including, of course, their plans for aggressive war."

The scenes were shocking. Gaunt, hollow-eyed prisoners stared at the camera. Bulldozers plowed naked bodies into trenches for burial. The film showed showers where victims expected to bathe but were instead murdered by poison gas seeping from fake showerheads. The camera focused in on torture rooms and on the incinerators where human bodies were burned.

Everyone in the courtroom was stunned by the gruesome images. Jackson noticed that many of the defendants looked shaken. Some even sobbed.

When the film ended, the Tribunal adjourned for the day. The room was silent. "Everybody wanted to get away from it," Jackson recalled. "It seemed as though the picture itself smelled of death and the sights and smells lingered with you."

A couple of weeks later, the Americans presented a second film as proof that the defendants plotted to wage war. *The Nazi Plan* was a collection of clips from Nazi propaganda movies, put together by Hollywood screenwriter Budd Schulberg and others.

The film started with scenes from 1921 when Hitler became the party's leader. It showed the defendants as they gathered for meetings and rallies. In the following scenes, the Nazis seized power in Germany, built up their war machine, and took over Europe. Once again, the Nazis themselves had created the evidence that the Allies used against them.

To prove that the Nazis planned to commit war crimes and crimes against humanity, the American team brought out documents signed by the defendants. The papers ordered the use of concentration camps as well as slave labor from occupied countries. Other papers recorded the number of Jews rounded up and killed in the concentration camps. At the Auschwitz concentration camp in Poland in July 1944, the Nazis murdered twelve thousand Jews a day.

On December 13, Thomas Dodd presented evidence found in a concentration camp—a section of human skin cut from a prisoner's body. He read testimony from a captured German soldier at the camp about how the Nazis made human skin into lampshades.

Nazi "Souvenirs"
When the American army seized the Buchenwald concentration camp in Germany in April 1945, soldiers found many grotesque objects created by the Nazis from the bodies of prisoners. These included shrunken human heads, parts of organs of victims who died of various diseases, tattoo markings on sections of human skin (in the foreground), and a lampshade made from skin of dead prisoners. American prosecutor Thomas Dodd presented some of this evidence at the Nuremberg Trial on December 13, 1945. The U.S. Army prepared this exhibit to show local German civilians the atrocities that had occurred in the camp next to their town.

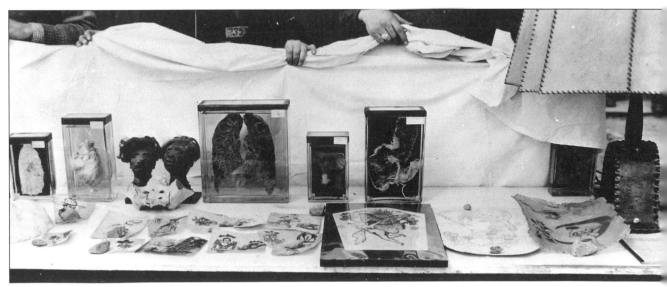

An assistant stepped to a small table covered with a white sheet. As he pulled off the sheet, Dodd said, "This exhibit ... is a human head with the skull bone removed, shrunken, stuffed, and preserved."

The spectators in the courtroom gasped.

Dodd went on, "The Nazis had one of their many victims decapitated, after having had him hanged ... and fashioned this terrible ornament from his head."

A few days after that chilling moment, the Tribunal adjourned for the Christmas recess. Everyone needed a break, including Jackson. He invited his staff to Lindenstrasse 33 for a turkey dinner and Christmas carols.

The break was too short for Jackson and Bill to make the long flight by propeller plane back to Washington for the holidays. They didn't want to take the risk of bad winter weather over the Atlantic Ocean delaying their return. Instead, they joined other staff members on a flight to the Mediterranean area, and they spent Christmas Eve in Bethlehem.

The trial was taking far longer than Jackson had anticipated. He wrote frequent letters home, "Dear Rene and Mary." After graduating from Smith College, Mary had married Thomas Loftus, a Navy doctor. She was pregnant and staying at Hickory Hill while her husband was stationed with remaining U.S. Navy forces in the Pacific.

Jackson told Irene and Mary how he had to disinfect the drinking water with chlorine tablets. He shaved by candlelight because they didn't have electricity most mornings. He complained about the scarce supplies and bad food.

During the next two months, the four Allied prosecution teams each presented part of the case against the Nazis. The French and Soviet prosecutors brought concentration-camp survivors to the witness stand. These former prisoners described conditions in the camps, including the filth, lack of food, torture, and murder.

Jackson spent hours in meetings with his team and with the other Allied prosecutors. They had to work out the details of the trial, coordinating their cases and sharing their evidence.

He wrote to Irene, "Every day I have to fight some kind of a fight with someone—Russians, French, the Tribunal, some of my staff, some meddlesome general. ... But we come out pretty well."

Jackson found time to get away from his trial work. With permission from the Army, he and Bill and an aide or two went hunting for deer and rabbits outside of Nuremberg. Of course, they always took along Jackson's bodyguard, Moritz Fuchs. When Fuchs shot a deer, Jackson felt reassured that his bodyguard had a good aim.

He hosted parties and dinners at Lindenstrasse 33. Elsie Douglas and Bill both liked to play the grand pianos that came with the house. Jackson encouraged guests to sing along. One of the other American prosecutors played violin, and he enjoyed having Bill or Elsie accompany him. Sometimes Bill played the bagpipes he'd bought during a short trip to London.

Jackson missed home, though. He was glad to get letters from Irene and Mary at Hickory Hill and from his sisters, Ella and Helen, in Frewsburg. "I keep thinking of the garden," he wrote in a letter, "and the ticks and dogs and all at home."

Hermann Goering on the witness stand in March 1946.

The trial dragged on into early March when the prosecution rested its case. Then each of the twenty-one men in the dock—including Kaltenbrunner, who had recovered from his stroke—had his turn to testify and call witnesses in his defense.

Hermann Goering went first. He spent four days on the witness stand, answering his German lawyer's questions. He had no apologies for bringing the Nazis to power. After he finished, the Allies got their chance to cross-examine him.

Jackson expected Goering to be a clever witness. When the Allies questioned him before the trial, he had skillfully avoided answering. Goering was conceited and considered himself far superior to the other defendants. Robert Jackson decided to use that vanity to pull admissions from him.

Goering sat in the witness stand across the room from Jackson's lectern.

Jackson began, "You are perhaps aware that you are the only living man who can expound to us the true purposes of the Nazi Party and the inner workings of its leadership?"

Wearing a smug smile, Goering leaned forward to speak into the microphone. "I am perfectly aware of that."

Jackson continued, "You, from the very beginning, together with those who were associated with you, intended to overthrow and later did overthrow, the Weimar Republic [the democratic German government from 1919–1933]?"

Goering didn't hesitate. "That was, as far as I am concerned, my firm intention."

"And, upon coming to power, you immediately abolished parliamentary government in Germany?"

"We found it to be no longer necessary," replied Goering.

Soon Goering turned his answers into long speeches. Jackson didn't want him to use the trial as a stage to spread Nazi propaganda, and he tried to stop the German. Jackson said to the judges, "I respectfully submit that the answers are not responsive, and I repeat the question."

It didn't help. Jackson's style was to pepper a hostile witness with rapid-fire questions, giving him no time to think up evasive replies. But the slight delays in translation broke up the rhythm of his cross-examination. Goering dodged the questions, and the judges let him give long answers.

Angry and frustrated, Jackson addressed the judges again. "This witness, it seems to me, is adopting ... in the witness box and

Listening to the Translation

As military police keep guard, the defendants listen to trial testimony, some through headphones. Two take notes, and one reads a book. Hermann Goering wears dark glasses to shield his eyes from the glare of bright camera lights.

in the dock, an arrogant and contemptuous attitude toward the Tribunal which is giving him the trial which he never gave a living soul, nor dead ones either."

For three days Jackson questioned Goering. Jackson felt that he hadn't received any help from the judges in controlling the Nazi. Finally, after Jackson challenged Goering with incriminating documents, the man's answers got shorter. By the time the cross-examination ended, Jackson thought that Goering had admitted to many crimes. Other observers believed that the wily Goering had outmaneuvered Jackson.

Jackson cross-examined other defendants. He was disgusted by the way they blamed everything on others who were—conveniently—dead or missing. Most claimed they were just following orders.

In April, Jackson said in a speech in Prague, "I have yet to hear one of these men say that he regretted he had a part in starting the war. Their only regret is at losing it."

Good news from home lifted his spirits and took Jackson's mind off the trial. In March, Mary gave birth to a son, Tommy. The proud grandfather wrote to Mary and Irene in May, "Tommy I suppose is making great progress. In fact from your description I should not be surprized [*sic*] to get a letter from him any time and am sure he walks and talks by now."

As spring came to Nuremberg, Bob Jackson planted vegetable seeds in the garden at Lindenstrasse 33. He had bought them during a trip to Paris. By June, the garden was producing spinach, lettuce, radishes, onions, and peas—a welcome change from canned food.

"But it isn't *my* garden," Jackson wrote to Irene and Mary. "I long to get my hand in our own soil and get the smell of the barn on my hands—I think I shall lie down with René [his horse] just to get the good old smell again."

⎯⎯⎯◈⎯⎯⎯

By the end of July, the lawyers for the defendants had summed up their cases. It was Jackson's turn to give his closing address. He had started working on the speech in January. "Since the first one went over so well," he wrote Irene and Mary, "I shall have to be particularly good this time or suffer an anticlimax."

The speech filled seventy pages of long white paper. Jackson had asked Elsie Douglas to type the final copy in large print so that he could read it easily as he spoke. She put wide spaces between lines. When he practiced the speech, Jackson underlined words that he wanted to emphasize, adding a double line for extra emphasis. He added slash marks where he wanted to pause.

On Friday morning, July 26, 1946, Jackson rose to give his closing address. He summed up the Americans' case, stressing that the trial had been conducted fairly. "They [the defendants] have been given the kind of a Trial which they ... never gave to any man."

Jackson looked toward the dock. "What these men have overlooked is that Adolf Hitler's acts are their acts. It was these men among millions of others, and it was these men leading millions of others, who built up Adolf Hitler. ... They intoxicated him with power and adulation. They fed his hates and aroused his fears. They put a loaded gun in his eager hands. It was left to Hitler to pull the trigger, and when he did they all at that time approved."

Leaving the Courtroom
Robert Jackson exits the courtroom, followed by son Bill in his U.S. Navy uniform. The white-helmeted military police maintained tight security at the courthouse.

Jackson reviewed how documents and the defendants' testimony proved their guilt. He attacked their claims of innocence. "They do protest too much. They deny knowing what was common knowledge. ... They deny even knowing the contents of documents they received and acted upon."

With an unwavering voice, he ended his speech. "These defendants now ask this Tribunal to say that they are not guilty of planning, executing, or conspiring to commit this long list of crimes and wrongs. ... If you were to say of these men that they are not guilty, it would be as true to say that there has been no war, there are no slain, there has been no crime."

The speech had gone as he had hoped.

Years later Sir Norman Birkett, the alternate British judge at Nuremberg, said of Robert Jackson's opening and closing addresses, "These two great speeches ... are the superb triumphs of his days at Nuremberg."

The British chief prosecutor, Sir Hartley Shawcross, wrote, "The plea of humanity to law could not have been expressed with greater power or to greater effect and that [opening] speech, as well as his closing address, will undoubtedly take their place in the history of international relations which they have done much to mould."

Jackson's role in the trial was finished. He had been away from Washington for more than ten months. It was time to go home.

⎯◆⎯

On the morning of October 1, 1946, an eager crowd lined up outside the Palace of Justice. Today the judges would read their verdict on the Nazi defendants. It was judgment day.

Security was tight. Soldiers surrounded the building, and everyone had to have a pass to get into the courtroom. The Army didn't want anybody staging a dramatic rescue of the prisoners.

Robert Jackson had returned to Nuremberg to hear the judges' decision. The day before, he had listened as the judges read the overall verdict. Today they would specifically address each defendant. Jackson took his seat at the American prosecution table with Bill and several of the other prosecutors.

Every chair in the press and visitor section was filled as the judges entered the courtroom. Starting with the presiding judge, Lord Geoffrey Lawrence, the four voting judges took turns reading the twenty-two defendants' names and the verdicts:

Goering, commander-in-chief of the air force, guilty of developing the Gestapo, creating concentration camps, persecuting Jews, and planning war.

Rudolf Hess, Hitler's deputy, guilty of planning aggressive war.

Joachim von Ribbentrop, minister of foreign affairs, guilty of participating in invasion plans and in deporting Jews in occupied countries.

Ernst Kaltenbrunner, chief of the security police, guilty of ordering the

Guilty
These three defendants were found guilty. Left to right: Rudolf Hess, Hitler's deputy, received life imprisonment; Baldur von Schirach, leader of youth, received twenty years; Joachim von Ribbentrop, minister of foreign affairs, was sentenced to hang.

murders and torture of civilians and prisoners of war and the extermination of millions of Jews.

Albert Speer, minister of war production, guilty of using civilian slave labor and Russian prisoners of war to make weapons.

When they reached the end of the list, Jackson was glad that the judges had found nineteen defendants guilty. Three men were acquitted: Franz von Papen, Hitler's vice chancellor and later a diplomat; Hans Fritzsche, the head of Nazi radio propaganda; and Hjalmar Schacht, a banker and the minister of economics until 1937. The judges did not think there was proof beyond a reasonable doubt that these men were guilty.

The Tribunal broke for lunch, and the guards led the defendants from the courtroom. When the court reconvened, the prisoner dock was empty. Lord Lawrence announced, "The International Military Tribunal will now pronounce the sentences on the defendants."

Jackson watched as a guard slid open the paneled door to the elevator behind the dock. Goering stepped into the courtroom. A guard handed him headphones.

Goering stood, waiting to hear the German translation of his sentence.

Lawrence said with a forceful voice, "Defendant Hermann Wilhelm Goering, on the Counts of the Indictment on which you have been convicted, the International Military Tribunal sentences you to death by hanging."

With no sign of emotion, Goering bowed slightly and then returned to the elevator.

The elevator returned to the ground floor for the second defendant. Next, Hess stepped into the courtroom.

Lord Lawrence continued, "Defendant Rudolf Hess, on the Counts of the Indictment on which you have been convicted, the Tribunal sentences you to imprisonment for life."

Guards brought the eighteen defendants into the courtroom, one at a time, to hear the judges' sentences. Twelve men were sentenced to death by hanging, including von Ribbentrop, Kaltenbrunner, and the missing Martin Bormann. Three of the Nazis received life in prison. Four, including Speer, received shorter prison terms ranging from ten to twenty years. Most of the defendants showed little emotion as they heard their fate.

At the end of Day 218, Lord Lawrence adjourned the International Military Tribunal for the last time.

Jackson was relieved. The Tribunal had held the defendants responsible for their horrible deeds. They had not gotten away with their excuse of merely obeying orders. Although Jackson was disappointed with the acquittals, at least these proved that the Allies had not rigged the trial to find the defendants guilty. It had been conducted fairly.

In his view, the Tribunal had confirmed for the first time in history that a war of aggression is a crime. The trial transcript and documentary evidence told the terrible, tragic story of how Hitler and the Nazis used their power to persecute people throughout Europe.

It was a lesson Jackson thought the world should learn. "Americans ought to be taught to recognize the early symptoms of such trends, for they can be checked only in their incipient stages."

Honored
In May 1947, the Jewish organization B'nai B'rith presented its Justice and Humanitarianism Award to Jackson for his role as chief American prosecutor at the Nuremberg Trial. Here he receives the award from the group's vice president at a ceremony in Washington.

The U.S. Army built three scaffolds in the jail gymnasium. In the early morning hours of October 16, ten Nazi leaders were hanged.

Missing was Hermann Goering. Death by hanging was too great a shame for him, a military man. A firing squad would have been more honorable. Hours before the scheduled hanging, Goering committed suicide in his cell by taking a cyanide capsule. No one ever learned how he obtained it.

Over the next three years in Nuremberg, the Americans conducted twelve more trials against nearly two hundred Nazis. The defendants included military leaders, judges, doctors, bankers, and businessmen. At the same time, the Allies held trials of Japanese leaders for war crimes they committed in Asia.

Others would prosecute these trials. On October 7, Robert Jackson resigned from his position as chief prosecutor, proud of what he had accomplished. "The hard months at Nuremberg," he later wrote, "were well spent in the most important, enduring, and constructive work of my life."

President Harry Truman wrote Jackson on October 17, 1946: "I am convinced that the verdict for which you worked will receive the accolade of civilized people everywhere and will stand in history as a beacon to warn international brigands of the fate that awaits them."

Telford Taylor succeeded Robert Jackson as chief prosecutor for the remaining Nuremberg trials. For nearly a year, he had watched Jackson organize the trial and prosecute the Nazi leaders. Taylor later said, "More than any other man of that period, Jackson worked and wrote with deep passion and spoke in winged words. There was no one else who could have done that half as well as he."

CHAPTER TEN

A Riot, a Strike, and an Eight-Year-Old Girl

While Robert Jackson was in Nuremberg, he missed an entire Supreme Court term. During his absence from the Court, he was pulled into a widely reported controversy, even though he was four thousand miles away.

On April 22, 1946, Chief Justice Harlan Stone collapsed in the courtroom and later died of a stroke. Jackson's friends in Washington telegrammed him in Nuremberg. They said that rumors were swirling about President Truman's choice to replace Stone. Jackson's name was being mentioned.

Jackson and Black
Robert Jackson and Hugo Black (right) had known each other for several years before serving together as associate justices on the Supreme Court. This photograph was taken in June 1937 when Assistant Attorney General Jackson testified before Congress in hearings about a wage and labor bill. Black (1886–1971) was then a Democratic senator from Alabama. President Roosevelt appointed Black to the Supreme Court two months later. On the left is Representative William Connery, Jr., of Massachusetts, who died two weeks after the photograph was taken.

Franklin Roosevelt had promised to make Jackson chief justice when Harlan Stone retired or died. Jackson and his supporters hoped that President Truman would follow through with Roosevelt's promise.

Soon Jackson heard that fellow justice Hugo Black was scheming to stop the president from choosing him. Sixty-year-old Black had been a lawyer before serving for ten years as Alabama's U.S. senator. FDR appointed him to the Supreme Court in 1937.

You need to be back here in Washington, Jackson's friends told him. He refused to go. The Nuremberg Trial was winding down, and he had important work left to do, including his closing address.

Then a Washington newspaper columnist wrote that Robert Jackson had a personal grudge against Hugo Black. Jackson figured that Black and his allies were behind the column. He couldn't ignore attacks on his character.

Jackson planned to tell President Truman that the ongoing feud in the Court was not about personal relationships, as the column claimed. Instead, it was about legal views and about Black's actions as a justice, which Jackson considered improper.

On June 6 Truman nominated Secretary of the Treasury Fred Vinson as chief justice. Perhaps the president realized that the Court had split with Jackson and Black on opposite sides. He needed to make a neutral choice rather than to appoint one of them.

A few days later, Jackson sent a cable to President Truman and the congressional judiciary committees. He accused Justice Hugo Black of voting in a case the year before in which Black's former law partner was one of the attorneys involved. Jackson charged that Black should have disqualified himself from the case and not tried to influence the vote of other justices.

Jackson wrote Irene a one-page note from Nuremberg: "I enclose a copy of a blunt and undiplomatic cable to the President. ... Of course this telegram will be regarded as only a gripe—but what the hell—the important thing is whether the Court is in someones [sic] pocket."

When people read the cable, they were taken aback. No Supreme Court justice had ever openly accused another of unethical actions. Disagreements on the Court usually stayed secret. Jackson had given the world a glimpse into the tensions among the justices. The *New York Times* said, "The quarrel was a severe blow to the court's prestige."

Senators, congressmen, and newspaper editorials suggested that both Jackson and Black should resign. Others said Jackson's outburst ended any consideration of him as a chief justice or presidential candidate.

Bob Jackson never regretted sending the cable. Several years later, he said, "I have every reason to feel that if I were in the same situation again, I would do just what I did, even though it brought a lot of criticism."

In the fall of 1946, Jackson returned to the Court for the new term. He wasn't sure how the publicized feud with Hugo Black would affect their relationship.

Black never spoke publicly about Jackson's cable. When the justices gathered for their first meeting in the fall, Black shook Jackson's hand right away as though nothing had happened.

After Vinson took his seat as chief justice, the controversy died away. Bob Jackson considered the rivalry with Black over. The two men were no longer competing for the chief justice position. They got along in person, even though they sometimes disagreed about Court matters.

Hitler at a Political Rally
In his Terminiello opinion, Justice Jackson quoted Nazi documents to show how Adolf Hitler had used public speeches to stir up hatred among the German public and to lead his country to war. In this photograph from 1923, Hitler addresses a crowd in Nuremberg, Germany, early in his political career.

Nuremberg had shown Robert Jackson how easily a dictator like Hitler could seize power. The lesson stayed with him when he returned to the Supreme Court. He was determined to protect each person's rights and freedoms from an overpowering government.

Yet Jackson didn't want the government to be so weak that it couldn't keep the country secure. Twice in his lifetime, he watched Germany take over Europe. Now Communist Soviet Union was moving to control the free countries in Eastern Europe.

In 1949, the Supreme Court heard a case involving both of Jackson's concerns.

Catholic priest Arthur Terminiello gave a political speech in a Chicago auditorium in February 1946. Outside, more than a thousand angry people protested against him. Shouting and cursing, they threw rocks at the auditorium windows and pounded on the doors.

Family Picnic
Robert Jackson with his family at Hickory Hill in 1950. Left to right: Irene; Jackson; nephew Harold Adams; sister Helen Jackson Adams; daughter Mary Jackson Loftus; and grandsons Thomas A. Loftus, III, and Robert H. Jackson Loftus. Eventually, Jackson and his wife would have eight grandchildren.

During his speech, Terminiello verbally attacked Jews and blacks and called former First Lady Eleanor Roosevelt a Communist. He urged his supporters to use violence against the "slimy scum" protestors.

Fights broke out between the two sides, and the police struggled to control the crowd. Afterward, they arrested Terminiello for encouraging the riot.

A Chicago jury found Terminiello guilty of disorderly conduct and fined him one hundred dollars. The priest appealed his case, saying the Constitution gave him the right of free speech. After the higher courts agreed with the original verdict against him, Terminiello appealed to the Supreme Court.

The Court heard arguments in the case, *Terminiello v. City of Chicago*. On May 16, 1949, the justices announced their decision in Arthur Terminiello's favor, voting 5–4 to overturn the verdicts of the previous courts. The majority said that the First Amendment protected Terminiello's freedom of speech. He shouldn't be punished just because his words stirred up the crowd.

Robert Jackson strongly opposed the majority's decision. In his twenty-four-page dissenting opinion, he said that Terminiello had the freedom to speak, even if his words were hateful. The important point was that the priest had used his speech to start a riot. Jackson quoted Nazi documents from the Nuremberg Trial to show that Hitler had done the same thing. The dictator gave speeches to large crowds, stirring up hatred in his listeners. That emotion led Germany to war and to the persecution of millions of innocent people.

Jackson wrote: "No mob has ever protected any liberty, even its own, but if not put down it always winds up in an orgy of lawlessness which respects no liberties."

He went on to write that the government needed the power of laws to prevent speakers from provoking violence. In his view, the Court's majority decision wrongly stopped Chicago from making such laws.

"The choice is not between order and liberty [of the citizen]. It is between liberty with order and anarchy without either. There is danger that, if the Court does not temper its doctrinaire logic with a little practical wisdom, it will convert the constitutional Bill of Rights into a suicide pact."

Many people agreed with Jackson's opinion, and it was quoted in newspapers across the country. The *New York Times* called it "eloquent."

In 1952, a showdown over presidential power occurred between the Supreme Court and President Harry Truman.

The United States had been fighting in Korea since the summer of 1950, when the Communist North Korean army invaded South Korea. The United Nations had called for its members to send troops to defend South Korea, and America deployed soldiers there.

In early 1952, the United Steelworkers union announced that they were going to strike for higher wages. A strike would shut down the nation's steel mills. President Truman didn't want that to happen, because the country needed steel to make weapons and other equipment for the Korean War.

Hours before the steelworkers planned to walk off the job, President Truman ordered Secretary of Commerce Charles Sawyer to take control of the steel mills. The government takeover stopped the workers from striking. Truman claimed that the Constitution gave him the power to act because of the Korean War.

The steel companies asked a federal court to end the government's control of their mills. They argued that Congress, not the president, had the constitutional

U.S. Commanders in Korea
In 1950, the United States sent troops to defend South Korea from Communist North Korea. General Douglas MacArthur (right) meets at the front lines with other U.S. military leaders in January 1951. MacArthur led the United Nations Coalition forces in Korea until April 1951, when President Truman relieved him of his military command for failure to follow Truman's orders.

right to take over a business in the interest of national security.

The lower court judge sided with the steel companies. He wouldn't let Secretary Sawyer keep control of the mills.

Sawyer appealed to the Supreme Court. The case was called *Youngstown Sheet & Tube Company v. Sawyer.*

Robert Jackson listened to the oral arguments and studied the case. When he served in Franklin Roosevelt's Justice Department, he supported the power of the president and the executive branch. But as a Supreme Court justice, Jackson had a duty to the law, not to a president.

He had seen what happened in Germany when a leader had the power to take over private property. Jackson thought President Truman had overstepped his constitutional authority, and it was the Court's responsibility to stop him. Jackson voted with the majority against the president.

On June 2, 1952, the Court announced the 6–3 decision: The Constitution did not give a president the authority to take control of private property without Congress's consent.

It took two and a half hours for seven justices to read their opinions in court. Three justices signed the single dissenting opinion, arguing that the president had such power during a crisis. The six majority justices each wrote separate opinions to explain why they restricted the president's authority.

In his concurring opinion, Robert Jackson wrote that Congress had refused to give the president this kind of power in previous situations. Congress had not said otherwise about the seizure of the steel mills. Therefore, Jackson assumed Congress did not intend for the president to have the authority in this situation either.

He laid out guidelines for deciding the limits of a president's power. The president had the most power when Congress supported his actions. The president's power was uncertain when Congress had not clearly approved or disapproved his action. Jackson called this "a zone of twilight." The president's power was "at its lowest ebb" when he acted against Congress's intentions. That was the case with the steel mills' seizure.

The strike was eventually settled without the nation's steel supply affected as seriously as Truman had feared.

The *Youngstown* decision limited presidential power after a period in which it had increased. During Roosevelt's administration, Congress and the Supreme Court had gone along with many of the president's decisions, especially during World War II. This ruling brought the three branches of government into balance again and became the basis for many later Court decisions.

In late 1952, the Supreme Court agreed to hear one of the most famous cases of Jackson's career as a justice.

Eight-year-old Linda Brown tried to enroll in the public

President Dwight Eisenhower
(1890–1969), a Republican, was elected president in 1952. During World War II, he was the Supreme Commander of Allied Forces in Europe.

Vinson Court
President Dwight Eisenhower welcomes the Supreme Court justices to the White House in February 1953. The Court had heard arguments in the Brown v. Board of Education case two months before. Front row, left to right: Justices William Douglas and Stanley Reed, Chief Justice Fred Vinson, President Eisenhower, and Justices Hugo Black and Felix Frankfurter. Back row, left to right: Sherman Adams, presidential assistant; Attorney General Herbert Brownell; and Justices Sherman Minton, Tom Clark, Robert Jackson, and Harold Burton.

elementary school seven blocks from her home in Topeka, Kansas. The school said Linda couldn't attend there because she was black. Only white students were allowed. Instead, Linda had to travel by bus to an all-black school twenty-two blocks away, a trip that took an hour and twenty minutes each way.

In 1950, Linda Brown was one of thousands of American children prohibited from attending their neighborhood school. Seventeen Southern states and Washington, D.C., had laws requiring public schools to separate by race.

Linda's father, Oliver Brown, and twelve other families joined in a lawsuit against the Board of Education of Topeka. Lawyers from the National Association for the Advancement of Colored People (NAACP) represented the families. They argued that separating schools by race was unconstitutional. The lawyers wanted the children to have a place in a school with both black and white students.

The lower court ruled against the Browns and the other families, saying that the black and white schools were equal. For that reason, the law that separated children by race was constitutional.

The NAACP appealed to the U.S. Supreme Court. The Court combined the Brown case with other cases that challenged school segregation laws in South Carolina, Virginia, and Delaware. The single case was called *Brown v. Board of Education of Topeka.*

The nine justices listened to oral arguments in December 1952. Afterward, they decided they weren't ready to rule yet. The justices asked the attorneys to answer more questions in briefs and to argue in court again, in the next term a year away.

Robert Jackson thought segregation was wrong. Black and white children should not be treated differently. Yet he wasn't convinced that the Supreme Court justices should be the ones to dictate such a major change in society.

Jackson believed the elected Congress or state legislatures should pass laws to end segregation. He didn't expect that to happen soon, though. Southern states were opposed to the laws, and their congressmen would surely stand in the way.

He knew that the Supreme Court didn't have the power to enforce its decision. Jackson wondered if Congress and the president would back up the

Court's ruling when school districts refused to stop segregating children.

By the next year, the Court had a new chief justice. Chief Justice Vinson had died in September. To replace him, President Dwight Eisenhower appointed Earl Warren, the Republican governor of California.

In December 1953, the Court held oral arguments on the *Brown* case again. Unlike the usual hour allowed for an argument, the Court listened to ten hours over three days. People camped outside the Supreme Court building so that they could get a seat in the courtroom.

Attorney John W. Davis, a former U.S. solicitor general, represented the state of South Carolina in the case. He argued that even though schools were separate, it didn't mean they were unequal. The states had the right to educate their children as they thought best.

NAACP attorney Thurgood Marshall argued for the families. He told the justices that segregating black and white children in schools was against the Constitution. To separate children by race made no sense. "They play in the streets together, they play on their farms together, they go down the road together, they separate to go to school, they come out of school and play ball together. They have to be separated in school."

Thurgood Marshall *(1908–1993) was the attorney for the NAACP in the* Brown v. Board of Education *case. Marshall later served as U.S. solicitor general. In 1967, he was appointed to the Supreme Court by President Lyndon Johnson, becoming the first African American to serve on the Court. This photograph was taken in 1957.*

Jackson made up his mind that the Court should reverse the 1896 Supreme Court ruling *Plessy v. Ferguson*. This decision had allowed separate but equal facilities for blacks. He worked on a draft of his legal view, expecting it to be a concurring opinion.

In a conference three months after the oral arguments, the majority of justices said they were ready to declare segregated schools unconstitutional. Chief

Justice Earl Warren would write the Court's opinion.

Then on Tuesday, March 30, 1954, Robert Jackson had a heart attack. His doctors sent him to the hospital to recover. They told him to cut back on his work and take it easy. Although he remained in the hospital for seven weeks, Jackson didn't stop working.

Chief Justice Warren visited him in the hospital to discuss the *Brown* case. Warren had been lobbying all of the justices to join in a single opinion.

Jackson listened as Warren explained why he wanted the Court's decision to be unanimous. Many people in the South will be angry about the ruling, the chief justice said. The decision will carry more weight if the nine justices speak with one voice.

He handed Jackson a draft of his opinion. It was only eleven pages long. Warren wanted the Court's opinion to be short so that the nation's newspapers would print all of it. It was important for people to read the opinion for themselves.

Jackson studied the opinion. Warren's arguments weren't exactly what he had used in his own draft. Still, he liked it. He thought the chief justice's opinion was powerful and written in language that everyone would understand.

Warren succeeded in getting all nine justices to agree to one opinion. The chief justice scheduled the announcement for mid-May.

Robert Jackson wanted to be sitting at the bench when Chief Justice Warren read the decision. The public should see the justices united behind it. His doctors advised him to rest longer, but Jackson went to the Court anyway.

On a sunny Monday afternoon, May 17, 1954, Jackson took his seat in the courtroom with the other eight Supreme Court justices. The word had gone out that an important decision would be announced. The courtroom was packed.

Chief Justice Warren read the decision: "We conclude unanimously that in the field of public education the doctrine of 'separate but equal' has no place. Separate educational facilities are inherently unequal."

Jackson watched the crowd as Warren read the opinion. Everyone seemed surprised when the chief justice spoke the word "unanimously." Most people expected the justices to split their decision.

The next day, newspapers around the country carried the headlines: "A 'Healing' Decision," "Milestone in Our History," "An Era Comes to End," "Decision Is Regretted," and "South Must Face Truth."

The *Brown* ruling was one of the Supreme Court's most well-known decisions. Yet it didn't end school segregation right away. As Robert Jackson feared, the Southern states resisted. More than twenty years passed before black and white students attended the same schools everywhere in the country.

———⊷∘⊶———

Throughout his career, Robert Jackson believed that judges should not use court opinions to force their political viewpoints on the country. In the 1930s, he had criticized the Supreme Court justices for striking down New Deal laws. He thought they had based their rulings on personal feelings about society, not on the Constitution. After thirteen years as a justice, Jackson still had the same view.

In most cases, Jackson thought the executive and legislative branches should decide the major changes in government and society. Elected officials were closer to the opinion of the people. If the public didn't like the changes, they could vote their representatives out of office.

But when the Supreme Court struck down a law or stopped a president's action, the nine justices had the last word. The nation had to live with the Court's decision, even if the justices made a mistake. For that reason, the Supreme Court had great power—and the responsibility to make decisions with extreme care.

Robert Jackson summed up his view in a 1953 court opinion: "We are not final because we are infallible, but we are infallible only because we are final."

CHAPTER ELEVEN

His Words Live On

October 9, 1954, was a warm and pleasant day in Washington. As Robert Jackson drove into the city that Saturday, he noticed a touch of autumn color on the leaves.

The first days of October had always been significant in Bob Jackson's life. Irene celebrated her birthday on the fifth. The new Court session started on the first Monday. His first day seated on the Supreme Court bench had been during this week in 1941. On the first of October in 1946, he had heard the Nuremberg judgment.

Since his heart attack in March, Jackson had both worked and relaxed. In July, he visited some old Jamestown friends and his sisters and their families in Frewsburg. He vacationed in California and went fishing in Canada with friends. But since he'd been back in Washington, the heat and humidity had made him feel more tired than usual.

On this morning, Jackson planned to run an errand. As he drove down a Washington street, he suddenly felt a sharp pain in his chest. He knew something was wrong.

Washington Funeral
Supreme Court guards carry Jackson's casket from the Washington National Cathedral after funeral services on October 12, 1954. Standing on either side of the doorway, the eight Supreme Court justices and the marshal and the clerk of the Supreme Court act as honorary pallbearers.

His secretary, Elsie Douglas, lived close by. He managed to drive to her home. She called his doctor immediately, but it was too late for anyone to help.

Shortly before noon, Robert Houghwout Jackson died of a heart attack.

On Monday, the Supreme Court met to pay tribute to Justice Jackson. A black cloth draped his empty chair. Chief Justice Earl Warren addressed the filled courtroom. "We shall miss greatly his wise counsel, his clarity of expression and his genial companionship."

The Empty Chair
Black crepe hangs in front of Robert H. Jackson's leather chair at the Supreme Court on the Monday after his death.

Jackson's calendar for Tuesday, October 12, showed an appointment with his doctor. Instead, at 3:00 that day, more than one thousand people attended his funeral at the Washington National Cathedral.

That evening, a train left for Jamestown, New York, with Robert Jackson's body. The eight Supreme Court justices traveled to New York with the Jackson family. In Jamestown, his body lay in state in St. Luke's Episcopal Church, where Bill had played the organ as a boy. Hundreds of people lined up to pay their respects. They had known Bob Jackson as he grew up in Frewsburg and practiced law in Jamestown. One longtime friend said, "Always in Jackson there was a lot of Frewsburg. ..."

He was buried later that Wednesday beside his parents in Maple Grove Cemetery, Frewsburg. Bob Jackson had come home.

His headstone reads: "He kept the ancient landmarks and built the new." The inscription sums up Jackson's life well. His Nuremberg bodyguard, Moritz Fuchs, who became a Catholic priest, later said that Robert Jackson was an example of "how even one person can have considerable influence for good in the world."

After his death, obituaries throughout the country recounted Jackson's many accomplishments. His hometown newspaper, the *Jamestown Post-Journal*, said

Grieving Family
The Jackson family—Irene, Bill, and Mary—arrive at the Washington National Cathedral for Robert Jackson's funeral. Nearly fifty years later, Bill's daughter Melissa said that her father never really got over Jackson's death and "grieved until the very day that he died." Mary's son Thomas described his mother's feelings for her father: "Grampa was our mother's superhero, and thus ours. His untimely death hit her extremely hard."

in an editorial, "The nation mourns a great statesman and jurist. ... But we in Jamestown, who have had the privilege to call him friend and neighbor, feel an even deeper grief. ... He was a man of homely character, true sincerity, wonderful friendliness and honest humility."

The *New York Times* noted, "Jackson ... will be remembered for the vigor, the incisiveness and the clarity of his thinking as a judge. ..."

The *Washington Post and Times Herald* praised Jackson's work in Nuremberg: "One of his great services to his generation was the prosecution of the Nazi war criminals. His opening statement and his summing up of the cases ... are not only powerful legal arguments but also masterpieces of English prose."

The Israeli ambassador Abba Eban sent Irene Jackson a condolence letter after Jackson's funeral. "The manner in which he defended the honor of the Jewish people in the Nuremberg trials will forever abide with us."

More than fifty years after Robert Jackson gave his closing speech, the International Military Tribunal remains a model for trials of war criminals. Recent tribunals have been organized to prosecute people accused of committing genocide in Rwanda, the former Yugoslavia, and Sierra Leone.

In 2002, the International Criminal Court was established, based on a treaty signed by more than one hundred nations. Located in The Hague, the Netherlands, the ICC was set up as a permanent court to investigate and try those who commit genocide and other war crimes. The ICC has investigated war crimes by leaders in Uganda, the Darfur region of Sudan, and the Democratic Republic of the Congo.

The United States is one of a number of countries that has not joined the ICC.

The nonmember countries are concerned about the extent of the ICC's power and the possibility that prosecutions will be politically motivated.

⬧—◆—⬧

As a Supreme Court justice, Robert Jackson wrote more than three hundred opinions. His words still apply to situations today. Since the terrorist attacks on September 11, 2001, Americans have debated the balance between citizens' rights and national security.

The issue in *Korematsu v. U.S.* was the World War II relocation of citizens in order to protect the West Coast from Japanese invasion. Today, some are concerned about the arrest of suspected terrorists based on race or ethnicity.

Other people fear that the government isn't doing enough to protect the nation from future attacks. They support increased surveillance of citizens. In their view, a terror attack could destroy the country, eliminating all freedoms. They sometimes quote Jackson's *Terminiello v. City of Chicago* opinion: "If the Court does not temper its doctrinaire logic with a little practical wisdom, it will convert the constitutional Bill of Rights into a suicide pact."

Many members of Congress want to restrict how far the president can go to protect the nation, especially without consulting them. Jackson's opinion in *Youngstown Sheet & Tube Company v. Sawyer* outlined the limits of presidential authority.

In the future, the Supreme Court may be asked to make decisions about similar cases. For this reason, the Senate wants to hear the views of Supreme Court nominees. During confirmation hearings, the senators have questioned nominees about Robert Jackson's opinions.

In 2006, the Senate Judiciary Committee held a hearing for President George W. Bush's nominee, Samuel Alito, who was later confirmed. Pennsylvania senator Arlen Specter asked Alito about the limits to the president's power. "I want to ... ask you first if you agree with ... Justice Jackson's concurrence in the Youngstown Steel seizure case."

Alito responded, "I do. I think it provides a very useful framework [for deciding limits]. And it has been used by the Supreme Court in a number of

important subsequent cases."

At John Roberts's September 2005 confirmation hearing for his nomination as chief justice, Vermont senator Patrick Leahy brought up Jackson's dissenting opinion in *Korematsu v. U.S.* Jackson had disagreed with the Court's majority, which said it was constitutional to keep a man away from the area where he lived based only on his race.

"I just want to make sure you're not going to be a Korematsu justice," Senator Leahy said to Roberts. "Can I assume that you ... would hold that to be unconstitutional?"

"I would be surprised if there were any arguments that could support it," replied Roberts, who was later confirmed.

Throughout the hearings, senators expressed admiration for Robert Jackson and his opinions. Senator Leahy called Justice Jackson one of his heroes.

John Roberts testified that Jackson was ranked with his favorite justices. Among other things, he admired Jackson's clear writing. "He was one of the best writers the court has ever had," Roberts told the senators. "You didn't have

Chief Justice Connection
Jackson with his law clerk William Rehnquist. Rehnquist (1924–2005) clerked for Jackson during 1952 and 1953 and became a Supreme Court associate justice in 1972. President Ronald Reagan appointed him chief justice in 1986, a position Rehnquist held until his death.

to be a lawyer to pick up one of his opinions and understand exactly what his reasoning is."

Although Robert Jackson never became chief justice, he is connected to a line of chief justices. His law clerk in 1952–1953 was

In 1981, Justice William Rehnquist (second from left) and his law clerks for the 1980–1981 Court term. On the right is John Roberts, who became chief justice in 2005.

William Rehnquist, who served as chief from 1986 to 2005. When Rehnquist died in 2005, *his* former law clerk John Roberts took the position.

Robert Jackson dedicated his life to the law, first as a lawyer, then as a judge. He believed that the basis of a government was its laws, not the whims of its leaders. Shortly before his death, he wrote: "There are only two real choices of government open to a people. It may be governed by law or it may be governed by the will of one or of a group of men. Law, as the expression of the ultimate will and wisdom of a people, has so far proven the safest guardian of liberty yet devised."

TIMELINE

1892 FEBRUARY 13—Born in Spring Creek, Pennsylvania.

1909 Graduates from Frewsburg (New York) High School.

1910 Graduates from Jamestown (New York) High School and begins apprenticeship in a Jamestown law office.

1911 Enters one-year program at Albany Law School.

1912 Receives certificate of graduation, Albany Law School.

1913 Admitted to the bar in New York State.

1914 July–AUGUST—**World War I begins in Europe.**

1916 Marries Irene Gerhardt.

1917 APRIL—**U.S. enters World War I.**

1918 NOVEMBER—**World War I ends with Germany's surrender.**

1919 Son William Eldred Jackson born.

1921 Daughter Mary Margaret Jackson born.

1929 OCTOBER—**New York Stock Market crashes. Great Depression begins.**

1932 NOVEMBER—**Franklin Delano Roosevelt (FDR) elected president of the U.S.**

1933 JANUARY—**Adolf Hitler becomes chancellor of Germany.**

1934 FEBRUARY—Appointed general counsel for Bureau of Revenue, Department of Treasury.

Adolf Hitler takes over as Germany's dictator.

1936 FEBRUARY—Becomes assistant attorney general, Tax Division, Department of Justice.

NOVEMBER—**FDR elected to second term as president.**

1937 JANUARY—Appointed assistant attorney general, Antitrust Division, Department of Justice.

1938 MARCH—Named U.S. solicitor general.

1939 SEPTEMBER—**Hitler invades Poland. France and Great Britain declare war against Germany. World War II begins.**

1940 JANUARY—Becomes U.S. attorney general.

JUNE—**France surrenders to the Germans.**

NOVEMBER—**FDR elected to a third term as president.**

TIMELINE

1941 JULY—Sworn in as associate justice of the Supreme Court.

DECEMBER 7—**Japan attacks Pearl Harbor, Hawaii. U.S. enters World War II.**

1943 JUNE—Supreme Court announces decision in *West Virginia State Board of Education v. Barnette.*

1944 NOVEMBER—**FDR elected to a fourth term.**

DECEMBER—Supreme Court announces decision in *Korematsu v. United States.*

1945 APRIL—**President Roosevelt dies. Vice President Harry Truman sworn in as president. Adolf Hitler commits suicide.**

MAY—President Truman appoints RHJ to be chief U.S. prosecutor in the trial against Nazi war criminals. **Germany surrenders. War in Europe ends.**

AUGUST— Allies sign the London Agreement, establishing the International Military Tribunal. **Japan surrenders. World War II ends.**

NOVEMBER—Nuremberg War Crimes Trial begins in Germany.

1946 APRIL—Chief Justice Harlan Stone dies while RHJ is in Nuremberg.

OCTOBER—Nuremberg Trial ends. Defendants are sentenced. RHJ returns to his duties at the Supreme Court after a one-year absence.

1949 MAY—Supreme Court announces decision in *Terminiello v. City of Chicago.*

1950 JUNE—**Communist North Korea attacks South Korea. Korean War begins. U.S. sends troops to defend South Korea.**

1952 JUNE—Supreme Court announces decision in *Youngstown Sheet & Tube Company v. Sawyer.*

NOVEMBER—**Dwight Eisenhower elected president.**

1953 **Fighting in Korea ends.**

1954 MARCH—Hospitalized after a heart attack.

MAY—Supreme Court announces decision in *Brown v. Board of Education of Topeka.*

OCTOBER 9—Suffers a fatal heart attack in Washington, D.C.

NOTES

The source of each quotation in this book is found below. The citation indicates the first words of the quotation and its document source. The sources are listed in the bibliography.

THE FOLLOWING ABBREVIATIONS ARE USED:

CUOHROC ("Reminiscences of Robert H. Jackson, 1955" Columbia University Oral History Research Office Collection)

IMT (Transcript of the International Military Tribunal found at the Web site *The Nuremberg War Crimes Trials*, Avalon Project, Yale Law School)

JC (Archives of the Robert H. Jackson Center)

RHJ Papers (Robert Houghwout Jackson Papers, Manuscript Division, Library of Congress)

CHAPTER ONE PAGE 9

"discords were ...": Jackson, *Report of Robert H. Jackson*, p. vi.

"a long, hard ...": CUOHROC, p. 1395.

"The privilege of opening ...": IMT, vol. 2, November 21, 1945, pp. 98–99.

"These prisoners ...": same as above, p. 99.

CHAPTER TWO PAGE 12

"I let out a cry ...": unpublished autobiography, RHJ Papers, box 189.

"As soon as my legs ...": CUOHROC, p. 10.

"We did as ...": draft of "Justice Jackson's Story," p. 27, JC.

"I had a pony ...": RHJ to Eugene Gerhart, Memo #2, January 1949, JC.

"more questions ...": Lena Jackson, quoted in Arch Bristow, *Erie* (PA) *Dispatch*, October 17, 1950.

"One of his hobbies ...": quoted in Lucian C. Warren, "Jackson's Home Town Proud But Bit Shocked," *Buffalo* (NY) *Courier-Express*, April 17, 1938.

"a perfectly normal boy ...": same as above.

"Enthusiastic student ...": RHJ Papers, box 244.

"My parents were busy ...": CUOHROC, p. 9.

"I spent much more time ...": CUOHROC, p. 22.

"I never hunted ...": CUOHROC, p. 42.

"he first voted for...": RHJ Papers, box 190.

"free-for-alls ...": CUOHROC, p. 50.

"They [the people] ...": RHJ Papers, box 190.

"I was always taught ...": same as above.

"I do not think ...": RHJ to Gerhart, Memo #2, January 1949, JC.

CHAPTER THREE PAGE 21

"He ... was not more ...": Judge Harley N. Crosby, quoted in Gerhart, *America's Advocate*, p. 32.

"distinctly the best ...": Samuel H. Edson, quoted in Warren.

"I was impressed ...": CUOHROC, pp. 60–61.

"He had a style ...": Earle Hultquist, "An Explanation of Jackson's Description in the 1910 *Red and Green*," JC.

"Why, Bob ...": quoted in CUOHROC, p. 63.

"You must not dare ...": letter from Mary Willard to RHJ, May 25, 1917, RHJ Papers, box 21.

"They had a fine collection ...": CUOHROC, p. 63.

"little Bob ...": letter from Mary Willard to RHJ, February 13, 1917, RHJ Papers, box 21.

"Her influence ...": CUOHROC, p. 64.

"I still hope ...": "Tribute to Milton J. Fletcher," June 30, 1932, JC, www.roberthjackson.org/Man/theman2-7-1-2.

"Quite a big fee!" and "You ... day.": CUOHROC, p. 67.

"Let it be ...": "An Unappreciated Heritage," Oration, June 21, 1910, JC, www.roberthjackson.org/Man/theman2-7-10-1.

"a life-long curiosity ...": "Address at Dedication of Jamestown High School Building," November 15, 1935, JC, www.roberthjackson.org/Man/theman2-7-2-1.

CHAPTER FOUR PAGE 27

"I hesitate ...": CUOHROC, p. 67.

"I thought I would ...": CUOHROC, p. 70.

"one of the most ...": CUOHROC, p. 71.

"He's too skinny ...": quoted in Adams, p. 1.

"until the day ...": CUOHROC, p. 97.

"You absorbed ...": CUOHROC, p. 75.

"Politically, he was ...": Jackson, *That Man*, p. 3.

"It was great ...": CUOHROC, p. 52.

"In his later life he marred ...": CUOHROC, p. 33.

"He never yielded ...": John Lord O'Brian, in Desmond, p. 8.

"I like the combat" and "When I see six ...": quoted in Gerhart, *America's Advocate*, p. 36.

"We tried the love life ...": CUOHROC, p. 77.

NOTES

"I tried to anticipate ...": CUOHROC, p. 83.

"I should hate ...": Harley N. Crosby, quoted in Gerhart, *America's Advocate*, p. 41.

"had a powerful ...": Samuel Edson, quoted in Warren.

"tune in ...": Ernest Crawcroft, quoted in Warren.

"Since my work ...": RHJ response to reporter's query, January 1939, quoted in Barrett, "Robert H. Jackson Email List Archive," February 12, 2007.

"I can't say ...": RHJ to Vesta Willard, July 1932, RHJ Papers, box 21.

Chapter Five page 37

"I consider that Mr. Mellon ...": Henry Morgenthau, quoted in Schlesinger, p. 569.

"I had a feeling ...": CUOHROC, p. 378.

"Germany was ...": CUOHROC, p. 380.

"After a 'war to end war'...": "Address at Dedication of Jamestown High School Building," November 15, 1935, JC, www.roberthjackson.org/Man/theman2-7-2-1.

"one of the nation's ...": "Round for Mellon," *Time*, May 24, 1937, Time Archive online, www.time.com/time/magazine/article/0,9171,848675,00.html.

"I wasn't a member ...": CUOHROC, p. 411.

"Jackson had a first-rate ...": Eliot, p. 26.

"I thought society ...": CUOHROC, p. 491.

"is the kind of man ...": Ickes, vol. 2, p. 262.

"The Court ...": quoted in Gerhart, *America's Advocate*, p. 115.

"This thing ...": same as above, p. 107.

"There is a serious lag ...": Jackson, "Reorganization of Federal Judiciary," statement before U.S. Senate Committee on the Judiciary, March 11, 1937, p. 26, JC, www.roberthjackson.org/Man/theman2-5.

"Honest 'Bob' ...": "Quiet Crisis," *Time*, March 22, 1937, Time Archive online, www.time.com/time/magazine/article/0,9171,757423,00.html.

Chapter Six page 47

"Bob, you can't leave ...": quoted in CUOHROC, p. 614.

"If you can be elected ...": same as above, p. 615.

"I told the President ...": unpublished autobiography, p. 128, RHJ Papers, box 189.

"It [the governorship]...": CUOHROC, p. 628.

"born for roughhouse ...": Ernest Cuneo, quoted in Lash, p. 352.

"one fault is that ...": Tom Corcoran, quoted in Ickes, vol. 2, p. 594.

"I said that Bob Jackson ...": Ickes, vol. 2, p. 395.

"the best spokesman ...": Ernest Lindley, "The New Dealers," *Washington Post*, August 27, 1939, p. B9.

"The only office ...": unpublished autobiography, p. 143, RHJ Papers, box 189.

"brains, nerve ...": "Small-town lawyer lifted to eminence in the New Deal may become political dynamite, but business doesn't understand him," *Fortune*, March 1938, p. 79.

"Jackson should be Solicitor General ...": Frankfurter, *Harvard Law Review*, p. 939.

"I made three ...": Jackson, "Advocacy Before the United States Supreme Court," p. 6.

"supremely confident ...": Gardner, p. 439.

"the most enjoyable ...": CUOHROC, p. 656.

"Bob Jackson ... stayed ...": Ickes, vol. 2, p. 628.

"Gentlemen, by noon ...": quoted by Jackson in *That Man*, p. 77.

"how long we could ...": CUOHROC, p. 1126.

"Thus I stepped ...": unpublished autobiography, p. 235, RHJ Papers, box 189.

"You might say ...": CUOHROC, p. 813.

"I couldn't see how ...": CUOHROC, p. 914.

"In the process of upholding ...": quoted in Meese, p. 779.

"The best thing about ...": quoted in Marsh, p. 41.

"He disliked the daily ...": Biddle, p. 99.

"I hope you don't get appointed ...": Mary Jackson to her parents, January 25, 1941, RHJ Papers, box 1.

"In New Deal circles ...": Ernest K. Lindley, "Picking a Successor to Hughes," *Washington Post*, June 8, 1941, p. B5.

"I think I will have ...": quoted by Jackson in CUOHROC, p. 1086.

"Associate justice ...": CUOHROC, p. 1086.

Chapter Seven page 59

"One must not judge ...": RHJ Papers, box 189.

"Justice Jackson treated ...": McLay, pp. 51–52.

"Although he seemed to write ...": Marsh, p. 47.

"Something does happen ...": CUOHROC, p. 1097.

NOTES

"other people's controversies ...": same as above.

"The first [world] war ... world.": CUOHROC, p. 127.

"I sputtered ...": CUOHROC, p. 1123.

"militant and thoroughly ...": Arthur Krock, "The Supreme Court at Its Peak," *New York Times*, June 15, 1943, p. 20.

"Bill of Rights ...": Jackson, *West Virginia State Board of Education v. Barnette*, 319 U.S. 624 (1943), p. 634.

"If there is any fixed star ... therein.": same as above, p. 642.

"one of the most notable ...": Arthur Krock, "The Supreme Court at Its Peak," *New York Times*, June 15, 1943, p. 20.

"I think the limits ...": Jackson, *Prince v. Massachusetts*, 321 U.S. 158 (1944), p. 177.

"The question ... majority.": Jackson, *The Supreme Court in the American System of Government*, p. 77.

"Korematsu ... resign.": Jackson, *Korematsu v. United States*, 323 U.S. 214 (1944), p. 243.

"then we may ...": same as above, p. 245.

"I do not think ...": same as above, p. 248.

"He wrote ... felt. His speech ... type.": Frankfurter, *Harvard Law Review*, p. 938, and *Columbia Law Review*, p. 437.

"May I be advised ... agree." and "That's the influence ...": quoted by Freund in Desmond, p. 34.

"I didn't realize ...": CUOHROC, p. 1094.

"No other event ... loss. We are ... Orient.": Jackson, *That Man*, pp. 167, 169.

CHAPTER EIGHT PAGE 70

"punish only the right ...": Jackson, *Report of Robert H. Jackson*, p. 46.

"Robert Jackson's ...": Biddle, p. 385.

"I can't go out ...": RHJ to Irene Jackson, n.d., RHJ Papers, box 2.

"We must establish ...": Jackson, *Report of Robert H. Jackson*, p. 48.

"I did not think ...": same as above, p. 211.

"It was a gross ...": Douglas, p. 28.

"I hope you had ...": RHJ to Irene Jackson, October 12, 1945, RHJ Papers, box 2.

"This is the first ...": Gordon Dean's preface to Jackson, *The Case Against the Nazi War Criminals*, 1946, p. xiii, quoted in Taylor, *The Anatomy of the Nuremberg Trials*, p. 503.

CHAPTER NINE PAGE 79

"Before I answer ...": IMT, vol. 2, 21 November 1945, p. 97.

"I informed ...": same as above.

"I declare myself ...": same as above.

"I will now call ...": same as above, p. 98.

"That four great ...": same as above, p. 99.

"We must never ...": same as above, p. 101.

"This war ...": same as above, p. 104.

"Of the 9,600,000 ...": same as above, p. 119.

"We have here ...": same as above, p. 142.

"The ultimate ...": same as above, p. 154.

"brilliant ...": "Nuernberg," *Washington Post*, November 23, 1945, p. 6.

"It is more than ...": letter from William Shirer to Jackson, RHJ Papers, box 109.

"We intend to prove ...": IMT, vol. 2, 29 November 1945, p. 432.

"Everybody wanted to ...": CUOHROC, pp. 1407–08.

"This exhibit ...": IMT, vol. 3, 13 December 1945, p. 516.

"The Nazis ...": same as above.

"Every day I have to ...": RHJ to Irene Jackson, n.d., RHJ Papers, box 2.

"I keep thinking ...": RHJ to Irene Jackson, May 3, 1946, RHJ Papers, box 2.

"You are perhaps ...": IMT, vol. 9, 18 March 1946, p. 417.

"I am perfectly aware ...": same as above.

"You, from the ...": same as above.

"That was ...": same as above, p. 418.

"And, upon ...": same as above.

"We found it ...": same as above.

"I respectfully submit ...": same as above, p. 455.

"This witness ...": IMT, vol. 9, 19 March 1946, p. 508.

"I have yet to hear ...": Jackson, *That Man*, p. 170.

"Tommy I suppose ...": RHJ to Irene Jackson and Mary Jackson Loftus, May 17, 1946, RHJ Papers, box 2.

"But it isn't ...": RHJ to Irene Jackson and Mary Jackson Loftus, June 22, 1946, RHJ Papers, box 2.

"Since the first one ...": RHJ to Irene Jackson and Mary Jackson Loftus, May 17, 1946, RHJ Papers, box 2.

"They [the defendants]...": IMT, vol. 19, 26 July 1946, p. 399.

"What these men ...": same as above, p. 424.

"They do protest ...": same as above, p. 427.

NOTES

"These defendants ...": same as above, p. 432.

"These two great speeches ...": Norman Birkett, foreword to *America's Advocate* by Gerhart, p. vii.

"The plea of humanity ...": quoted in Gerhart, *America's Advocate*, p. 516.

"The International ...": IMT, vol. 22, 1 October 1946, p. 588.

"Defendant Hermann ...": same as above.

"Defendant Rudolf ...": same as above.

"Americans ought to be ...": Jackson, preface to *The Nürnberg Case*, p. x.

"The hard months at Nuremberg ...": Jackson, introduction to *Tyranny on Trial* by Harris, p. xxxvii.

"I am convinced ...": Truman to Jackson, October 17, 1946, "The War Crimes Trials at Nuremberg," Truman Library & Museum, www.trumanlibrary.org/whistlestop/study_collections/nuremberg/documents/index.php?documentdate=1946-10-17&documentid=2-7&studycollectionid=&pagenumber=1.

"More than any other ...": Taylor, *The Anatomy of the Nuremberg Trials*, p. 634.

Chapter Ten page 95

"I enclose a copy ...": RHJ to Irene Jackson, early June 1946, RHJ Papers, box 2.

"The quarrel ...": "The Nation," *New York Times*, June 16, 1946, p. E1.

"I have every reason ...": CUOHROC, p. 1600.

"slimy scum": Terminiello quoted by Jackson in *Terminiello v. City of Chicago*, 337 U.S. 1 (1949), p. 17.

"No mob has ever ...": Jackson, *Terminiello v. City of Chicago*, 337 U.S. 1 (1949), p. 32.

"The choice is not between ...": same as above, p. 37.

"eloquent.": "The Terminiello Decision," *New York Times*, May 21, 1949, p. 12.

"a zone of twilight" ... "at its lowest ebb": Jackson, *Youngstown Sheet & Tube Company v. Sawyer*, 343 U.S. 579 (1952), p. 637.

"They play in the streets ...": quoted in "The Tension of Change," *Time*, September 19, 1955, Time Archive online, www.time.com/time/magazine/article/0,9171,865192,00.html.

"We conclude ...": Earl Warren, *Brown v. Board of Education*, 347 U.S. 483 (1954), p. 495.

"A 'Healing' Decision ...": quoted in "Editorial Excerpts from Nation's Press on Segregation Ruling,"

New York Times, May 18, 1954, p. 19.

"We are not final ...": Jackson, *Brown v. Allen*, 344 U.S. 443 (1953), p. 540.

Chapter Eleven page 106

"We shall miss ...": quoted in "Court Eulogizes Justice Jackson," *New York Times*, October 12, 1954, p. 27.

"Always in Jackson ...": Charles S. Desmond, in Desmond, p. 23.

"how even one ...": Father Moritz Fuchs, "Robert H. Jackson Memorial Service," October 3, 2004, Jamestown, New York, JC, www.roberthjackson.org/Man/Speeches_About_50thAnniversary_MemorialService/.

"The nation mourns ...": "Nation Loses Great Statesman and Jurist in Jackson Death," *Jamestown* (NY) *Post-Journal*, October 11, 1954.

"Jackson ... will be ...": "Justice Jackson," *New York Times*, October 11, 1954, p. 26.

"One of his great ...": "Robert H. Jackson," *Washington Post and Times Herald*, October 11, 1954, p. 14.

"The manner ...": Abba Eban to Irene Jackson, October 14, 1954, RHJ Papers, box 6.

"grieved until ...": Melissa Jackson, Dedication of Jackson Center, Jamestown, NY, May 16, 2003, www.devo.buffalo.edu/streaming/dedication.htm.

"Grampa was our ...": Loftus, p. 40.

"If the Court ...": Jackson, *Terminiello v. City of Chicago*, 337 U.S. 1 (1949), p. 37.

"I want to ...": U.S. Senate Committee on the Judiciary, *Hearing on Nomination of Samuel A. Alito, Jr., to be an Associate Justice of the Supreme Court*, 109th Congress, 2nd session, January 9, 2006.

"I do. I think ...": same as above.

"I just want to make ...": U.S. Senate Committee on the Judiciary, *Hearing on Nomination of Judge John G. Roberts, Jr., to be Chief Justice of the Supreme Court*, 109th Congress, 1st session, September 13, 2005.

"I would be surprised ...": same as above.

"He was one of the best ...": same as above, September 14, 2005.

"There are only two ...": Jackson, *The Supreme Court in the American System of Government*, p. 27.

BIBLIOGRAPHY

Abraham, Henry. "Mr. Justice Robert H. Jackson (1892–1954): An Attempt to Place Him into Some Historical Perspective." Remarks, Robert H. Jackson Center, Jamestown, NY, March 18, 2003. www.roberthjackson.org/Man/theman2-6-15.

Adams, Harold Jackson. "A Tribute to Robert Jackson by his Nephew." *Albany Law Review* 68, no. 1 (2004): 1–3.

Barrett, John Q. "Albany in the Life Trajectory of Robert H. Jackson." *Albany Law Review* 68, no. 3 (2005): 513–37.

———. "A Commander's Power, A Civilian's Reason: Justice Jackson's Korematsu Dissent." *Law and Contemporary Problems* 68 (Spring 2005): 57–79.

———. "Justice Robert H. Jackson on Security, Liberty and Law." Chautauqua Institution lecture, July 23, 2003. The Robert H. Jackson Center Lecture Series Podcast. www.procasts.com/?podcastID=28.

———. "Robert H. Jackson Email List Archive." St. John's University School of Law. www.stjohns.edu/academics/graduate/law/faculty/profiles/Barrett/JacksonList.sju.

Biddle, Francis. *In Brief Authority*. Garden City, NY: Doubleday, 1962.

Cushman, Barry. *Rethinking the New Deal Court: The Structure of a Constitutional Revolution*. New York: Oxford University Press, 1998.

Cushman, Clare, and Melvin I. Urofsky, eds. *Black, White, and* Brown: *The Landmark School Desegregation Case in Retrospect*. Washington, DC: Supreme Court Historical Society, 2004.

Davis, Kenneth S. *FDR, Into the Storm, 1937–1940: A History*. New York: Random House, 1993.

Desmond, Charles S., Paul A. Freund, Potter Stewart, and Lord Shawcross. *Mr. Justice Jackson: Four Lectures in His Honor*. New York: Columbia University Press, 1969.

Domnarski, William. The *Great Justices 1941–54: Black, Douglas, Frankfurter & Jackson in Chambers*. Ann Arbor: University of Michigan Press, 2006.

Douglas, William O. *The Court Years, 1939–1975: The Autobiography of William O. Douglas*. New York: Random House, 1980.

Dunne, Gerald T. *Hugo Black and the Judicial Revolution*. New York: Simon and Schuster, 1977.

Eliot, Thomas H. *Recollections of the New Deal: When the People Mattered*. Boston: Northeastern University Press, 1992.

Fassett, John David, Earl E. Pollock, E. Barrett Prettyman, Jr., and Frank E. A. Sander. "Supreme Court Law Clerks' Recollections of *Brown v. Board of Education*." *St. John's Law Review* 78 (2004): 515–67.

Fourteenth Census of the United States Taken in the Year 1920. Vol. 1. Washington, DC: United States Bureau of the Census, 1921.

Frankfurter, Felix. "Foreword." *Columbia Law Review* 55 (April 1955): 435–37.

———. "Mr. Justice Jackson." *Harvard Law Review* 68 (April 1955): 937–39.

Gardner, Warner W. "Government Attorney." *Columbia Law Review* 55 (April 1955): 438–44.

Gerhart, Eugene C. *America's Advocate: Robert H. Jackson*. Indianapolis: Bobbs-Merrill, 1958.

———. *Supreme Court Justice Jackson: Lawyer's Judge*. Albany: Q Corporation, 1961.

Halpern, Philip. "Robert H. Jackson, 1892–1954." *Stanford Law Review* 8 (December 1955): 3–8.

Harris, Whitney R. *Tyranny on Trial: The Trial of the Major German War Criminals at the End of World War II at Nuremberg, Germany, 1945–46*. Dallas: Southern Methodist University Press, 1999.

BIBLIOGRAPHY

Harry S. Truman Library and Museum. Independence, Missouri. www.trumanlibrary.org.

Hockett, Jeffrey D. *New Deal Justice: The Constitutional Jurisprudence of Hugo L. Black, Felix Frankfurter, and Robert H. Jackson.* Lanham, MD: Rowman and Littlefield, 1996.

Ickes, Harold L. *The Secret Diary of Harold L. Ickes.* Vols. 2 and 3. New York: Simon and Schuster, 1954.

Jackson, Robert H. "Advocacy Before the United States Supreme Court." *Cornell Law Quarterly* 37 (Fall 1951): 1–16.

———. *Dispassionate Justice: A Synthesis of the Judicial Opinions of Robert H. Jackson.* Edited by Glendon A. Schubert. Indianapolis: Bobbs-Merrill, 1969.

———. *The Nürnberg Case, as Presented by Robert H. Jackson, Chief Counsel for the United States, Together with Other Documents.* New York: Cooper Square Publishers, 1971. First published 1947 by Alfred A. Knopf.

———. *The Reminiscences of Robert H. Jackson.* Edited by Harlan B. Phillips. Columbia University Oral History Research Office Collection, 1955.

———. *Report of Robert H. Jackson, United States Representative to the International Conference on Military Trials, London, 1945.* Washington, DC : Department of State, 1949.

———. *The Struggle for Judicial Supremacy: A Study of a Crisis in American Power Politics.* New York: Alfred A. Knopf, 1949.

———. *The Supreme Court in the American System of Government.* Cambridge, MA: Harvard University Press, 1955.

———. *That Man: An Insider's Portrait of Franklin D. Roosevelt.* Edited and introduced by John Q. Barrett. New York: Oxford University Press, 2003.

Jackson, Robert Houghwout. Papers. Manuscript Division, Library of Congress, Washington, DC.

Jamestown (NY) *Evening Journal.* January 18, 1897, through December 12, 1911.

Kilmuir, The Right Honourable Viscount (David Maxwell Fyfe). "Justice Jackson and Nuremberg—A British Tribute." *Stanford Law Review* 8 (December 1955): 54–59.

Kurland, Philip B. *Politics, the Constitution, and the Warren Court.* Chicago: University of Chicago Press, 1970.

———. "Robert H. Jackson." In *The Justices of the United States Supreme Court 1789–1969: Their Lives and Major Opinions,* vol. 4, edited by Leon Friedman and Fred L. Israel, 2541–90. New York: Chelsea House, 1969.

Lash, Joseph P. *Dealers and Dreamers: A New Look at the New Deal.* New York: Doubleday, 1988.

Leuchtenburg, William E. *Franklin D. Roosevelt and the New Deal, 1932–1940.* New York: Harper and Row, 1963.

———. *The Supreme Court Reborn: The Constitutional Revolution in the Age of Roosevelt.* New York: Oxford University Press, 1995.

Loftus, Thomas A., III. "That Baby: Justice Jackson's Writings about a Grandchild, and Vice Versa." *Albany Law Review* 68, no. 1 (2004): 37–40.

Marsh, James M. "The Genial Justice: Robert H. Jackson." *Albany Law Review* 68, no. 1 (2004): 41–49.

McKean, David. *Tommy the Cork: Washington's Ultimate Insider from Roosevelt to Reagan.* Hanover, NH: Steerforth Press, 2004.

McLay, Alma Soller. "That Twinkle in His Eyes." *Albany Law Review* 68, no. 1 (2004): 51–53.

BIBLIOGRAPHY

McMahon, Helen G. *Chautauqua County, A History.* Buffalo, NY: Henry Stewart, 1958.

Meese, Edwin, III. "Robert H. Jackson, Public Servant." *Albany Law Review* 68, no. 4 (2005): 777–81.

Morrison, Wayne E., Sr., ed. *A History of Chautauqua County, New York, 1808–1874.* Ovid, NY: W. E. Morrison, 1969.

"The Nuremberg Trials." VHS. Produced and directed by Michael Kloft. *American Experience.* PBS Home Video, 2006.

The Nuremberg War Crimes Trials. The Avalon Project at Yale Law School. www.yale.edu/lawweb/avalon/imt/imt.htm.

Persico, Joseph E. *Nuremberg: Infamy on Trial.* New York: Viking, 1994.

Pritchett, C. Herman. *The Roosevelt Court: A Study in Judicial Politics and Values, 1937–1947.* New York: Macmillan, 1948.

Ransom, William L. "Associate Justice Robert H. Jackson." *American Bar Association Journal* 27 (August 1941): 478–82.

Rehnquist, William H. "Robert H. Jackson: A Perspective Twenty-Five Years Later." *Albany Law Review* 44 (April 1980): 533–41.

———. *The Supreme Court.* New York: Alfred A. Knopf, 2001.

"Resolutions in Honor of the Memory of the Late Associate Justice Robert Houghwout Jackson of the Supreme Court of the United States." Prepared by the Committee on Resolutions Appointed by Solicitor General of the United States Simon E. Solbeloff. October 1954. Robert H. Jackson Center. www.roberthjackson.org/Man/Speeches_aboutRHJ_SCResolutions.

Robert H. Jackson Center. Jamestown, New York. www.roberthjackson.org.

Rodell, Fred. *Nine Men: A Political History of the Supreme Court from 1790 to 1955.* New York: Random House, 1955.

Schlesinger, Arthur M., Jr. *The Age of Roosevelt: The Coming of the New Deal.* Boston: Houghton Mifflin, 1959.

Schubert, Glendon A. *Constitutional Politics: The Political Behavior of Supreme Court Justices and the Constitutional Policies That They Make.* New York: Holt, Rinehart and Winston, 1960.

———. *The Judicial Mind: The Attitudes and Ideologies of Supreme Court Justices, 1946–1963.* Evanston, IL: Northwestern University Press, 1965.

Shaw, Stephen K., William D. Pederson, and Frank J. Williams, eds. *Franklin D. Roosevelt and the Transformation of the Supreme Court.* Vol. 3. Armonk, NY: M. E. Sharpe, 2004.

Sonnenfeldt, Richard W. Radio Interview, *The Leonard Lopate Show.* WNYC, November 9, 2006.

———. *Witness to Nuremberg.* New York: Arcade Publishing, 2006.

Stone, Geoffrey R. *Perilous Times: Free Speech in Wartime from the Sedition Act of 1798 to the War on Terrorism.* New York: W. W. Norton, 2004.

Taylor, Telford. *The Anatomy of the Nuremberg Trials: A Personal Memoir.* Boston: Little, Brown, 1992.

———. "The Nuremberg Trials." *Columbia Law Review* 55 (April 1955): 489–525.

Urofsky, Melvin I. *Division and Discord: The Supreme Court under Stone and Vinson, 1941–1953.* Columbia: University of South Carolina Press, 1997.

Urofsky, Melvin I., and Paul Finkelman. *A March of Liberty: A Constitutional History of the United States.* Vol. 2., 2nd ed. New York: Oxford University Press, 2002.

BIBLIOGRAPHY

Watkins, T. H. *Righteous Pilgrim: The Life and Times of Harold L. Ickes, 1874–1952*. New York: Henry Holt, 1990.

White, G. Edward. *The American Judicial Tradition: Profiles of Leading American Judges*. 3rd ed. New York: Oxford University Press, 2007.

Yoder, Edwin M., Jr. *The Unmaking of a Whig and Other Essays in Self-Definition*. Washington, DC: Georgetown University Press, 1990.

The following periodicals are cited in the Notes:

Buffalo (NY) *Courier-Express*

Erie (PA) *Dispatch*

Fortune

Jamestown (NY) *Post-Journal*

New York Times

Time Magazine Archive Online

Washington Post

Washington Post and Times Herald

FOR MORE INFORMATION*

ON ROBERT HOUGHWOUT JACKSON

Robert H. Jackson Center, Jamestown, New York. www.robertjackson.org.

Read Jackson's judicial opinions and articles. Listen to his recorded speeches. Watch interviews with his family, friends, and colleagues.

ON THE ADMINISTRATIONS OF PRESIDENTS WILSON, HOOVER, ROOSEVELT, TRUMAN, AND EISENHOWER

Woodrow Wilson Presidential Library, Staunton, Virginia. www.woodrowwilson.org.

Herbert Hoover Presidential Library and Museum, West Branch, Iowa. www.hoover.archives.gov.

Franklin D. Roosevelt Presidential Library and Museum, Hyde Park, New York. www.fdrlibrary.marist.edu.

Harry S. Truman Library and Museum, Independence, Missouri. www.trumanlibrary.org.

Dwight D. Eisenhower Presidential Library and Museum, Abilene, Kansas. www.eisenhower.utexas.edu.

Library Web sites contain information about each president's life and administration, including documents, speeches, and photographs. Sites have student sections with additional research sources.

ON THE SUPREME COURT

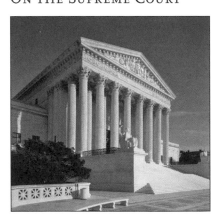

Supreme Court of the United States, Washington, D.C. www.supremecourtus.gov.

The official Web site includes history of the Supreme Court, biographies of the justices, information about recent cases and Court procedures. The Court building is open to the public. Take a tour, listen to oral arguments, and watch the justices in action.

The Supreme Court, PBS series. www.pbs.org/wnet/supremecourt.

Features history of the Court and its notable decisions, interviews with justices, and lists of print and online resources.

*Web sites active at time of publication

FOR MORE INFORMATION

Supreme Court Historical Society.
www.supremecourthistory.org.

Gives overview of the Court's history and traditions, with special sections on landmark cases, including *Korematsu v. U.S.* and *Brown v. Board of Education.*

U.S. Supreme Court Center.
www.supreme.justia.com.

Contains the complete text of Supreme Court rulings. Includes links to commentary and blogs about the Court.

Oyez Project.
www.oyez.org.

A multimedia archive of the U.S. Supreme Court. Take a virtual tour of the Supreme Court building. Listen to selected oral arguments.

Legal Information Institute, Cornell University Law School.
www.law.cornell.edu/supct/index.html.

Provides text of Supreme Court decisions, both historic and current.

The Brown Foundation.
www.brownvboard.org.

Features information about the 1954 *Brown v. Board of Education* decision.

On the Nuremberg War Crimes Trial

Avalon Project at Yale Law School.
www.yale.edu/lawweb/avalon/imt/imt.htm.

Contains the complete transcript of the International Military Tribunal at Nuremberg.

"The Nuremberg Trials," *American Experience.*
www.pbs.org/wgbh/amex/nuremberg/.

Web site for the PBS program provides timeline, photographs, and lists of World War II books and Web sites.

Famous Trials.
www.law.umkc.edu/faculty/projects/ftrials/ftrials.htm.

Includes an account of all Nuremberg trials, 1945–1949, by Douglas O. Linder, professor of law at the University of Missouri–Kansas City School of Law. Has links to additional resources.

United States Holocaust Memorial Museum, Washington, D.C.
www.ushmm.org.

Features extensive information about the Holocaust, including the doctors' trial at Nuremberg. Lists research sources.

International Criminal Court.
www.icc-cpi.int.

Discusses the ICC's history, organization, and recent cases.

INDEX

Page numbers in **boldface** refer to photographs.

Albany, New York, 28–29, 32
Alito, Samuel, 109, **110**
Biddle, Francis, **55**, 74, **81**
Birkett, Norman, **81**, 91
Black, Hugo, **52**, 67, 68, 78, **95**, 96–97, **101**
Bormann, Martin, 81, 93
Brandeis, Louis, 50, 51, 59
Brown v. Board of Education of Topeka, 101–105, 113, 123
Bryan, William Jennings, **22**, 22–23, **33**
Chautauqua Institution, 22, **31**
Chautauqua Lake, 23, 35, **42**
Churchill, Winston, **70**, 71
Concentration camps, **71**, **84**, 84–86, **85**, 91
Davis, John W., 103
Dean, Benjamin, 27
Destroyers for Bases Agreement, 54, **54**
Dodd, Thomas, **82**, 84–86
Douglas, Elsie, 75, **82**, 87, 90, 107
Douglas, William, 51, **52**, 68, 78, **101**
Eisenhower, Dwight, **101**, 103, 113, 122
Fletcher, Milton, 25, **25**, 26
Frankfurter, Felix, **52**, 67, **101**
Frewsburg, New York, 14–23, **18**, **29**, 32, 39, 106, 107
Fritzsche, Hans, 92
Fuchs, Moritz, 76, 87, 107
Goering, Hermann, 77, **78**, 80, 81, 82, **87**, 87–89, **88**, 91, 92–93, 94
Great Depression, 10–11, **35**, 35–37, **37**, 39, 44, 112
Hess, Rudolf, 77, **78**, 91, **92**, 93
Hickory Hill, 59–62, **61**, 68, 86, 87, **98**
Hitler, Adolf
    rise to power, 41, **41**, 75, **78**, 82, 85, **97**, 98, 112
    and World War II, 52–55, 70, 71, 77, 90, 112–113
Hoover, Herbert, 36, **36**, 39, **46**, 122
Houghwout, Parthena (grandmother), 17, **17**
Hughes, Charles Evans, 22, 46, **46**, **52**, 57
Ickes, Harold, 44, **48**, 49, 51
International Criminal Court, 108–109, 123
International Military Tribunal. *See* Nuremberg War Crimes Trial
Jackson, Angelina Houghwout (mother), 12, 13, **13**, **16**, **19**, 27, 28, **29**, 42
Jackson, Elijah (great-grandfather), 12, 13, 58
Jackson, Ella (sister), 13, **16**, **19**, 32, **42**, **63**, 87
Jackson, Helen (sister), **16**, 17, **19**, **29**, 32, **42**, **63**, 87, **98**
Jackson, Irene Gerhardt (wife)
    birthday, 78, 106
    courtship and wedding, 28–29, 32, **32**, 112
    Jackson's funeral, **108**

INDEX

Jamestown family life, 34–39, **35**, **42**, **60**
    letters from Jackson in Nuremberg, 76, 78, 86–87, 89, 96
    in Washington, D.C., **51**, **53**, **57**, **58**, 59–60, 62–63, 68–69, **98**
Jackson, Mary Eldred (grandmother), 16, 17
Jackson, Mary Margaret (daughter)
    childhood and youth, 34, **34**, **35**, 47, 51, 56, **57**, **58**, **60**, 112
    children, 89, **98**
    Jackson's funeral, **108**
    letters from Jackson in Nuremberg, 86–87, 89
Jackson, Melissa (granddaughter), **108**
Jackson, Nancy Roosevelt (daughter-in-law), 75
Jackson, Robert Houghwout, 112, 113
    Antitrust Division, Justice Department, 42, 44–49, **95**
    apprenticeship, 27, 29–30
    associate justice, Supreme Court, 10–11, **57**, 57–71, **58**, **59**, **61**, 78, 95–105, **101**,
        109–111, **111**, **122**
    attorney general, Justice Department, 11, 53–57, **55**, **56**, 100
    Bureau of Revenue, Treasury Department, 38–41
    chief American prosecutor at the International Military Tribunal
        See London Conference; Nuremberg War Crimes Trial
    chief justice position, 57–58, 62, 95–97, 110–111
    childhood and youth, 12–26, **16**, **19**, **22**, **24**, **26**
    children. *See* Jackson, Mary Margaret; Jackson, William Eldred, "Bill"
    court-packing bill, 44–46, **45**
    death and funeral, **106**, 106–107, **107**, **108**
    education
        Albany Law School, 28
        Frewsburg School, 15, **15**, 19–23, 26
        Jamestown High School, **23**, 23–26, **26**
    grandchildren, 89, **98**, **108**. *See also* Jackson, Melissa; Loftus, Thomas A., III
    health, 56, 104, 106
    Hugo Black, feud with, 95–97
    law career, private practice, 29–38, 50
    marriage, 32, **51**, **53**, **60**. *See also* Jackson, Irene Gerhardt
    Mellon tax case, 39–41
    New York politics, 30–31, **31**, 47–48, **49**
    Roosevelt, relationship with, 10, 30, **31**, 36–37, 39, 42, 44–58, **48**, **58**, 62, 68–69, 96
    solicitor general, Justice Department, 49–51, **52**
    Tax Division, Justice Department, 42
    Washington, D.C., move to, 38–39, 59
Jackson, Robert Rutherford (grandfather), **17**, 17–18, **19**, 21
Jackson, William Eldred (father), 12–16, **14**, **16**, **19**, 27, 28, **29**, 32
Jackson, William Eldred, "Bill" (son)
    assistant to Jackson at Nuremberg, 72, 75, 80, 86, 87, **90**, 91
    childhood and youth, **34**, **35**, 38, 47, 51–52, 56, 58, **58**, **60**, 107, 112
    Jackson's funeral, **108**
Jackson, William Miles (great-uncle), 13, 14, 17
Jamestown, New York, 23–26, **27**, 29–35, 38–39, 41, 42, 45, 52, 53, 56, **60**, 63, 78, 106, 107

INDEX

Japanese internment camps, 65–67, **66**, 109
    See also *Korematsu v. U.S.*
Jehovah's Witnesses, 63–65, **64**
    See also *West Virginia State Board of Education v. Barnette*
Judicial review, 43
Kaltenbrunner, Ernst, 77–78, 80–81, 87, 91–92, 93
Korean War, 99–100, **100**, 113
Korematsu v. U.S., 65–68, 109, 110, 113, 123
Lawrence, Lord Geoffrey, **81**, 81–82, 91–93
Leahy, Patrick, 110
Lend-Lease Act, **56**, 56–57
Loftus, Thomas A., Jr. (son-in-law), 86
Loftus, Thomas A., III (grandson), 89, **98**, **108**
London Conference, **72**, 72–74
Marshall, Thurgood, 103, **103**
Mellon, Andrew, **39**, 39–41
Morgenthau, Henry, Jr., 38, 39
Mott, Frank, 27–32, **31**
Nazi Party, 9, 10, **41**, 70–78, **78**, 80–94, 98
New Deal, 10, 36, 38–39, 41, 44–46, 49, 50, 105
Nuremberg, Germany, **8**, 9–10, **41**, **74**, 74–76, **75**, **78**, 87, 89, 94, 95, **97**
Nuremberg War Crimes Trial, 113, 123
    courtroom, **11**, 75, **75**, **76**, **79**, **81**, 81, **82**, **90**
    defendants, 10, 77–81, **81**, **82**, **87**, 87–89, **88**, 91–94, **92**
    evidence, 9, **73**, 77, 82–86, **83**, **84**, **85**, 98
    Jackson's closing address, 89–91, 108
    Jackson's cross-examination of Goering, 87–89
    Jackson's opening address, 9–10, 80, 82–83, 108
    judges, 73–74, 80–82, **81**, 87–89, 91–92
    Palace of Justice, **75**
    translation system, 10, 76–77, **77**
    verdict, 91–94
Parker, John J., 81
Rehnquist, William, 111, **111**
Roberts, John, **110**, 110–111, **111**
Roosevelt, Franklin Delano
    assistant secretary of Navy, **30**
    court-packing bill, 44–46
    death and funeral, 68–69, **69**, 113
    elections, 36, **36**, 42, 45, 56, 112–113
    governor of New York, **31**, 36
    Jackson, relationship with, 10, 30, **31**, 36–37, 39, 42, 44–58, **48**, **58**, 62, 68–69, 96
        See also under Jackson, Robert Houghwout
    president of U.S., 36–42, 44–58, 62, **62**, 66, **70**, 101, 112–113, 122
    Supreme Court appointments, 46, 51, 53, 57, **58**, 68
Roosevelt, Theodore, 22, 76
Rosenman, Samuel, 70
Schacht, Hjalmar, 92

INDEX

Specter, Arlen, 109

Speer, Albert, 77, 92, 93

Spring Creek, Pennsylvania, 12, **12**, 13, 14, 58, 112

Stalin, Joseph, **70**, 71

Stone, Harlan, **52**, 57, 58, 59, 71, 78, 95, 96, 113

Terminiello v. City of Chicago, 97–99, 109, 113

Truman, Harry, 69–72, **71**, 74, 77, 78, 94, 95–96, 99–101, 113, 122

U.S. Supreme Court

    building, **50**, **122**

    Jackson arguing before, 42, 49–50

    justices, **46**, 51, **52**, 53, 57, **101**, 102, 103, **103**, **104**, 104–105, **106**, 107, **110**, 110–111, **111**

    New Deal era, 44–46

    organization and procedures, 43, 59, 109, 122

    See also under Jackson, Robert Houghwout

Vinson, Fred, 96, 97, **101**, 103

Von Papen, Franz, 92

Von Ribbentrop, Joachim, 76, 91, **92**, 93

Von Schirach, Baldur, **92**

Warren, Earl, 103–105, **104**, 107

West Virginia State Board of Education v. Barnette, 63–65, 68, 113

Willard, Mary, 24–26, 36

Willard, Vesta, 25, 36

Wilson, Woodrow, 30–32, **33**, 122

World War I, 31–32, **32**, 33, 34, 41, 112

World War II

    in Asia, 61–62, **62**, 65-68, **66**, 74, 94, 113

    Destroyers for Bases Agreement, 54, **54**

    destruction and casualties, **8**, 9, 61–62, **62**, 71, **71**, 73–75, **74**, **84**, 84–86, **85**

    in Europe, 51–57, 62, 68, 70–73, 112–113

    Lend Lease Act, **56**, 56–57

    Neutrality Acts, 41, 54

    Pearl Harbor attack, 61, **62**, 113

    preparations for, 53–57, **54**, **55**

    U.S. declaration of war, 62, **62**

    Victory Gardens, 62

    Yalta Conference, **70**

    See also concentration camps; Hitler, Adolf; Japanese internment camps; Nuremberg War Crimes Trial

Youngstown Sheet & Tube Company v. Sawyer, 99–101, 109, 113

PICTURE CREDITS